MW01204489

It's a Process

Discovering Purpose in this Crazy World

Noah Dean, PhD

To my wife, Lauren.

#WarriorQueen

CONTENTS

PREFACE

"It's not supposed to be this way."

Those scathing words echoed in my mind. Like a software glitch, they wouldn't stop affirming the same, obvious truth over and over. It was déjà vu of a tormenting sort. I had been here before, but not like this... not at this age.

I stormed over to the computer. I was angry, and I wanted to document the injustice. I wanted the world to know. However, reality wasn't what I thought it was. Over the next several months, as I wrote, my perspective began to develop. I progressed—*gradually*—from the bitter child to a devoted student. It was a slow but necessary process to what would, ultimately, yield refreshing forgiveness and an unprecedented peace. What began as an immature endeavor of animosity transitioned to something completely different.

In retrospect, the echoes had been right. I wasn't supposed to be broken, lost, and defeated. But that was my event horizon—the point at which I began to tear away from the despair.

It's a Process is a story of a divinely inspired escape. Perhaps it can help you as well.

IT'S A PROCESS

Everyone has his own specific vocation or mission in life; everyone must carry out a concrete assignment that demands fulfillment. Therein he cannot be replaced, nor can his life be repeated, thus, everyone's task is unique as his specific opportunity to implement it.

— *Man's Search for Meaning*, Viktor Frankl

IT'S A PROCESS

INTRODUCTION

It's in Your Hands

When I was a boy, I was convinced that turning forty years old marked a significant point in one's life—the absolute pinnacle. I had heard the cliché "over the hill", and believed that forty indicated the time of peak expertise, where wisdom and capability were maximized to a point that every day afterward was a sad display of slow, agonizing deterioration. However, when I reached the four-decade mark, I felt nowhere near accomplished, wise, or capable; but I did feel the decay. Soon after my 40th birthday, I found myself trudging through unemployment, depression, and a waning sense of purpose. It seemed I had summited that hill much earlier than expected, or somehow teleported to the bottom of the other side.

Eventually, I became mindful of the truth. I managed to find the path God had arranged for me—and the hill no longer mattered. It is this awareness that I hope to spark within you.

It's a Process is an appeal to those struggling with a fading resolve. It is my sincere effort to teach, guide, and encourage anyone who may be experiencing *agonizing deterioration*—those craving betterment and hope.

This book is a resource to not only illustrate the importance of applying the various reviewed lessons, but also inspire continual learning. All the points outlined in *It's a Process* require a consistent determination for development—an ongoing effort to manage influences, overcome adversities, and act on a trust that we each have a divinely inspired place in this crazy world. The themes herein will overlap, too. There are explicit links, inter-chapter highways that bring various points together. It is your responsibility as the reader to consider these connections and meditate on how the topics build upon, rely on, and weave throughout each chapter. Doing so will inspire critical thought, self-reflection, and hopefully, a permanent change in perspective.

But no author can do this for you. The potential for improvement relies entirely on the one you see in the mirror.

So buckle up, it's a process.

CHAPTER 1

HONESTY

Don't lie about anything, ever.

— Jordan Peterson

The Shot

I gazed into the mirror, my eyes locked onto the jagged cross that was shoddily painted on my forehead. The blood had dried by now, and what was once a red, shimmering symbol of victory had darkened into a maroon, cracked shadow of its former self. My smile had faded too. I couldn't fake excitement anymore. Confusion consumed me. Was I a hunter? Had I solidified my place in the world as a man? Or had I been tricked, lied to? I was caught between two supposed truths that offset one another, a paradox that my nine-year-old mind couldn't resolve.

I closed my eyes and replayed it all in my head.

I had yanked the trigger—and failed to gently "squeeze" it as I had been told. I was aiming for her torso. The first

3

shot, my shot, boomed from the .30-30 lever-action rifle that I held firmly against the tree branch. Alarmed, her head launched upward from the cool creek water, eyes desperately searching to identify the direction of the threat. But there was no more time. When the deafening explosion from Mr. Taylor's rifle sounded, her face instantly vanished, morbidly shattering into a pink mist. A violent, chaotic reaction ensued as what was left of her nervous system continued to force violent muscle contractions throughout her body. The result was a grotesque display of kicking, jerking, convulsing ... dying. Finally, she fell still. As I approached, the damage became painfully clear. A fragmented, distorted mass of flesh and bone—saturated in varying shades of red—demanded my attention. Visible were bits and pieces not designed to be seen. To one side, a dislodged eye hung from what little remained of her face. For a young boy, it was what nightmares are made of.

She was looking at me, speaking to me. She was asking the same question I was. Had her death mattered?

I abandoned my reflection in the mirror and returned to the living room where the men had all gathered, including Mr. Taylor. Days before he had promised my mother that he would take me deer hunting, a request she had made to help fill the void of a father's absence. He had fulfilled his commitment earlier that day by taking me to the riverbank, handing me the lever-action rifle, then pointing a gun of his own at the unwitting doe. On my head, he had then drawn the congratulatory cross with the warm blood from the sacrificial deer, a symbol of a *first kill*.

Mr. Taylor was a large man with a wide face and a thick gray beard. I approached him—a young boy addressing a mountain.

"If I was the one who shot the deer, why was there a pause?" I asked.

He glanced at the distorted cross on my head and then, looking into my eyes, muttered "What do you mean?"

I spoke slowly, aligning my words with the rerun playing in my mind. "After I fired a shot, there was a pause. But when you shot, she was hit."

He hesitated. "That was the delay," said Mr. Taylor. "That was the time it took your bullet to get there. *You* shot her."

I wanted to believe him. I wanted my first kill. I wanted to answer her, to tell her it was my doing, and that her death wasn't in vain. I wanted that violent, horrific memory—and the blood on my forehead—to mean something. But it didn't. Mr. Taylor was lying and I knew it. He was the one with the kill.

But I was used to lies; by that point in my life, I had been conditioned to them.

Isaac

My parents' divorce, which took place when I was an infant, initiated a seemingly endless ebb and flow of establishing and abandoning home bases. This connected my nomadic mother and me to multiple families, cities, and relationships—a pattern that continued throughout my childhood. One of the more persistent stops was with the relatively well-to-do Dorset family, who lived on an enormous mountain range ranch nestled just outside of Fort Davis, Texas. Not long before my hunting experience, my mother and I had moved to the ranch for a second time—this time with another divorce in the books. Nancy Dorset and her husband, John, once again offered to house us in one of the ranch's extra living quarters until we got back on our feet. It didn't take long for their son, Isaac, to reveal his feelings on the matter.

Born exactly one week before me, Isaac was one of the most malicious, deceitful human beings I would ever know. He was a frightful bully, an inexorable liar, and brilliantly manipulative, all exacerbated by his knowledge that he had the upper hand regarding our home life (or lack thereof). I vividly remember an event from one of those many days on the ranch. One afternoon, after moseying around outside, I walked into the main residence, strolling by the iconic front sink that every ranch house has, used to rid one's hands and arms of dirt, blood, grease, manure, and whatever else. As I passed it, I noticed a half dozen or so jellybeans sitting suspiciously on its forest-green tiled counter. Of all the places in that house to find candy randomly positioned, this particular sink was the most bizarre. I paused for a moment, contemplating throwing the delicious-looking rainbow assortment down the hatch. However, after considering the potential consequences—and delving deep into a whispering hint of warning—I cautiously stepped away and went on with my day. Only a few minutes had passed before I heard Nancy's bellowing voice echo throughout the house.

"Noah! Get in here!" As I approached the sink, there stood Nancy, right next to where the jellybeans *had* been.

"Did you eat those jellybeans?" she asked.

"No ma'am," I said timidly.

"Did you eat those jellybeans?!" she asked again, now more aggressively.

"No ma'am," I said again.

She was less than impressed, and quickly transitioned from accusation to fervent anger: "DID YOU EAT THOSE JELLYBEANS?!"

At that moment, I knew what I was in—and was surprised I hadn't realized it sooner. I was in the same hole I had been in dozens of times before, a trap set by none other than Isaac. Throughout my time in that hellacious household, I had been accused (and convicted) of starting fights, lying, stealing, cheating, and vandalism (once in the form of spreading multiple, slimy boogers all over a bathroom wall). All such episodes were brilliantly orchestrated by Prince Isaac himself. But he didn't stop at petty pranks. I had seen him, on multiple occasions, sexually violate his own grandmother, and physically abuse his intellectually disabled half-brother. Even today, I'm rather certain I've never met anyone more sinister. The jellybean trap was a minor offense for Isaac. But at that instant, he wasn't on trial—I was.

In the moment, literally standing in Nancy's domineering shadow, I only knew one way out. I had to lie.

"Yes," I said, "I ate the jellybeans."

Nancy lifted her head and looked down at me over the top of her nose. It was clearly the answer she had been waiting for, hoping for. She let out a deep, lasting sigh—and then walked away, which I was very thankful for. It was common for her to grab my frail arm and dig her sharp fingernails into my skin while viscously spewing callous words of anger into my terrified face. An uneventful exit was more than welcomed.

As an adult, I see how trivial those snares were, but for a young kid with nowhere else to go, it became torturous. It was a hell that could not be escaped, being locked in a prison of lies. But that was life, and I learned something extraordinarily valuable from it: how damaging lies can be— which made me despise their use.

I became a resolute fan of truth.

The Problem with Deception

Learning the Lesson

Isaac had shown me the dark power of deceit. He was able to manipulate others in ways that seemed almost miraculous, wielding a Godless magic that could snuff out the truth like a gust of wind overwhelming a candle's flame. He used lies to direct others toward a conclusion of his choosing, making my life unbearable.

The day my mother excitedly told me that I would "live forever" as a Christian, I started crying and couldn't stop. We were still living with the Dorset's and, to my young mind, that might mean living with them forever. I wanted no part of being lied about, bullied, and tormented *forever*. I certainly didn't want perpetually bruised arms.

And therein lies the wonderful lesson. Unbeknownst to Isaac, his constant, malicious attacks ultimately taught me the *truth* about how destructive lies can be. This helped me reject them later in life. Like a witness to the testing of a nuclear weapon, I saw firsthand the destructive power of hateful deceit—and wanted nothing to do with it. Unfortunately, I had to be at ground zero to learn such lessons. But they were learned, nonetheless. We're *all* releasing our own atom bombs of deceit … and we are *all* at ground zero, too.

White Lies

We lie. It's what we do—to avoid consequence, to build rapport, to garner wealth, to embellish, to trick, to manipulate, to get the girl or guy—we lie. We release small, trifling deceptions because we feel like the truth is somehow insufficient, or it's not entertaining enough, or we don't appear as important if we reveal mundane, simple, everyday truths. We seize opportunities to enhance, even just slightly, in order to appear a bit more interesting, noticeable, worthy. Lies are a tool that we use to falsely project ourselves as being more than we are. And we start young, too. We know what it means to rob someone of the truth early in life, and if not addressed, we can continue thieving well into adulthood.

One misconception is that a lie, even a small one, only *temporarily* misdirects. We tell ourselves that it doesn't really matter, that the victim of our deceit is no worse for wear. This is how we justify *half-truths* which, of course, require little to no regard for the other person. After all, it's just a "white lie," right?! That's what Mr. Taylor offered me. He told me that he, not I, had shot and killed the doe, fully convinced that his delicate lie wouldn't be that big of a deal. He may have even considered it charity, hoping to instill the excitement of victory within a young boy. We do this often. We use small falsehoods to dodge conversations, like answering "nothing" when our spouse probes us with "what's wrong?" We might exaggerate, even slightly, how much something costs, how far away something is, how much something hurts (or doesn't). We convince ourselves that there isn't enough weight in our lie for the misdirection to be consequential. Like Mr. Taylor, we embrace *charitable lies* too, like telling our children about Santa Claus, the tooth fairy, or a creepy leprechaun at the end of a rainbow.

Granted, direct earth-shattering consequences may not result from denying the truth about how hungry you are at a family reunion, whether you're a Billie Eilish fan, or where Santa Claus lives. But even if we don't consider the *implicit* damage of habitually telling half-truths, they *can* be damaging to others. Like a small splinter wedged in our skin, a sliver of a lie can cause big pain. Sometimes there are long-term consequences—whether we ever realize it or not.

Of course, lies can cut more like a battle axe than a splinter, and the damage they do can reveal much.

Carrying the Wound

Lies can be weapons. Isaac knew this. As much as they were meant to wound me, his deceptions were for his gain as well. In the case of the jellybeans, Isaac wanted to relish my being wounded—and labeled a thief and liar—while the halo around his head shined brighter. Many people feel the need to aggrandize, or even completely fabricate a story. Even in the most nonthreatening situation, some people find it tempting to tell a "white lie" for humor, to impress, to hurt, or sometimes for no reason at all! Sometimes we just find it better to deceive than to endure a minor inconvenience. This tendency illuminates the depths of human foolishness. It's not worth the trade-off. Small lies can serve as a gateway drug to bigger ones—a slippery slope to the depths of immorality, a vice that desensitizes a person to the unscrupulous art of dishonest misdirection. Just like every professional was once an amateur, every big lie started with a small one.

Lies echo. They project further and faster than many can imagine. But unlike echoes, which fade, lies can amplify over time, causing continued destruction. In some situations, the deep cut left by the lie remains an open wound. As time goes by, and if not properly dressed, the situation festers. One injured by lies will be tempted to adopt the same habit of deception. This is why marriages crumble, parents and children can't reconcile, and friends become enemies. It's why trusting others is, for many, so difficult. Unfortunately, many people in this world live with these invisible, gaping lesions. They are the *walking wounded*, and passing those lacerations onto others, eliciting problem after problem.

Perhaps you have experienced this yourself. You know what it means to bear wounds left by those who have used lies as a weapon, and now you have difficulty trusting others because of it. Maybe you have even *adopted* the use of lies yourself (although it requires advanced maturity to admit to it).

Whether victim or perpetrator, it's important that those affected by lies shake off the betrayal, leave the past behind, and let the wound heal. Yes, being hurt hurts. It took decades for me to forgive those who surrounded me at the Dorset ranch. But, in the end, I did forgive—and applied the lessons learned. The damage left by lies can be healed, but the injured party must act as the healer—the patient must also be the doctor.

Why do so many people live the life of the walking wounded? Why do we put ourselves in positions to be tricked and lied to by the "godless magic" spewed from others?

Answer: Because we're wired that way.

Default to Truth

I was first introduced to the concept of "default to truth" from reading Malcolm Gladwell's *Talking to Strangers*, a phenomenal book that examines our interactions with the unfamiliar people in our lives. In short, *default to truth* or "truth-default theory" is the idea that, when people consider the information others are communicating to them, they typically show unquestioned acceptance. In other words, when we are interacting with someone, we typically assume they're telling the truth. Interestingly, our "default to truth" tendency occurs even when a mountain of evidence suggests that the truth is *not* being told. Call it gullibility, denial, or both—it's just what we do.

If there was ever a soul that personified "default to truth," it was me. Despite my difficult years with Isaac, I have always been astoundingly gullible. I can tell dozens of stories in which my tendency to assume honesty in others resulted in disaster in some shape or form. Perhaps you, too, find yourself on the naive side of the spectrum.

Some deduce that our tendency to believe others is genetic, a survival trait that allows us to act decisively on what we're told and avoid danger. Although I've been bamboozled by a falsehood on many occasions, I'm proud of the fact that I lean toward believing others, be it forged by genetics, or otherwise. A propensity to trust others is a pillar of healthy optimism. Living in a constant state of skepticism and paranoia makes for an existence even more miserable than living with the scars of betrayal. Even though we may sometimes find ourselves on the wrong end of a lie, we should make a habit of trusting anyway. We need to embrace our natural tendency to default to truth.

However, assuming honesty in others is one thing—always *being* honest ourselves is something else entirely.

Living Honestly
Living with a firm commitment to honesty is not easy. In fact, it's terribly difficult at times! It often goes against our inherent inclinations. Most people, even those who consider themselves fervently honest, will be tempted to cast a fib or

two on a daily basis. Even Mother Nature is no stranger to liars. How many animals will pretend to be something other than themselves to avoid becoming a meal or getting one of their own? The Gaboon Viper pretends to be a pile of leaves, the Pygmy Seahorse camouflages itself as a piece of coral, the Dresser Crab glues random objects on itself to blend in with the ocean floor, and the Mimic Octopus transforms itself to look like *dozens* of other things. Our world is absolutely saturated with deception! It's important to know, however, that there's a difference between deceptive *animals* and deceptive *humans*.

Blending in with an environment to survive is one thing, but blatant dishonesty rooted in ego, pride, arrogance, or malice is very different. The Christian Bible holds numerous verses that warn against lying. But it's important to not just read "You shall not bear false witness …" and make a half-hearted attempt to comply. It's imperative that we understand the consequences of deception, even those minor infractions we have classified as "white lies." If one understands the catastrophic effects, they may be more willing to prevent the primal cause. This is what Isaac did for me. I experienced the torment of lies, lived through the consequences, and now have an incredibly clear perspective on the importance of honesty. I know how damaging lies can be.

Health and Relationships

> *Oh, what a tangled web we weave,*
> *When first we practise to deceive!*

— *Marmion: A Tale of Flodden Field,* Walter Scott

It's important to know that there are hidden consequences that reach beyond the damage experienced by those on the other side of lies. While it may not always be apparent, the *wielder* is hurt, too. The sharp blade of deceit cuts both parties.

Trust is the foundation of all human connections, the cornerstone of what brings people together. Habitual liars can often struggle to maintain long-lasting, quality relationships. Being a perpetual victim of lies inhibits trust; it often becomes too much of a burden to bear. Eventually, the victim distances themselves to prevent further deceit. Just like a cherished vase can only be broken and repaired so many times, so too do friends and family members reach a point of no return. Trust, or lack thereof, has a half-life.

But sadly, this is a hard habit to quit. The more one lies, the more those lies build on one another. The perpetrator feels the need to double down, then the lies are compounded to align stories, to save face. For example, a person may lie about where they've been, then feel forced to lie about what they were doing, where they were going, and who they were with. The first fib, meant to temporarily distract, ultimately results in an onslaught of deception. And then, to fully commit to it all, the liar must remember all the deceptive details to maintain the elaborate story! A sharp memory becomes necessary to maintain credibility, even when there is no real credibility at all. It's messy! Lying is like a dangerous drug—the more one uses it, the worse it gets.

Lying is easy—managing the consequences is not.

If you tell the truth, you don't have to remember anything.

—— Mark Twain

Biblical Review

Creating the Wedge

The Holy Bible is saturated with insight regarding the avoidance of deceit. Even for non-Christians, the wisdom regarding truth and lies within its pages is invaluable. I want to elaborate on two verses, each taken from what have become known as *wisdom books*.

A false witness will not go unpunished, and whoever pours out lies will perish.

—— Proverbs 19:9

While this may sound slightly dark, perhaps even sinister, the point is not that a liar will be ruthlessly struck by a lightning bolt hurled by an angry deity. It refers to the wedge that we create between the life God has outlined for us and the one we make for ourselves when we lie. It means that when we deceive, we inhibit ourselves from living out our divine purpose. God is truth (John 14:6), and when we deceive, God is unknown to us—we have turned our backs to Him with confidence that He's not needed. A *life* without God is the *death* of our purpose. However, God is very much needed if we hope to live out the perfect purpose that He's outlined for us. Lies are an incredibly effective form of self-sabotage.

However, this doesn't mean that *all* those who
perpetually lie will openly suffer. Sometimes, it seems like the
"bad guy" does pretty well and the "nice guy" really does
finish last. A liar won't always wallow in shame; the honest
person won't always win. Another wisdom book of the Bible
illuminates this paradox:

> *There is something else meaningless that occurs on*
> *earth: the righteous who get what the wicked deserve,*
> *and the wicked who get what the righteous deserve.*
> *This too, I say, is meaningless.*

— Ecclesiastes 8:14

That's right—sometimes the bad guy wins, and the good
guy doesn't get the girl. Sometimes the Isaacs in our lives
seem to live carefree, while we are left bruised and bloodied
by the slash of someone's sharp fingernails. This is what life
is at times—there's no way around it. We're imperfect people
living in an imperfect world. But it's not our job to categorize
what other people do or the "success" we feel they are having
or not having. Our job is to uphold a moral standard and
trust that we're better off, to refrain from being a "false
witness" and focus on being the person God has called us to
be.

It's better to experience the temporary frustrations that
might come from honesty than the provisional rewards that
might come from deceit.

17

Therefore each of you must put off falsehood and speak
truthfully to your neighbor,
for we are all members of one body.

—— Ephesians 4:25

The Solution

Avoid the Temptation

Friends, fight the urge to embellish. How often have we added a bit of flair to a story, only to realize that the little extra, the exaggeration, added nothing of significance?

We should avoid, to the greatest extent we can, deviations from the truth. We should steer clear of "white lies" that are the building blocks for greater, more damaging falsehoods.

Those who think it is permissible to tell white lies soon
grow color-blind.

— Austin O'Malley

By eliminating petty, insignificant exaggerations, we will start to see our very character develop. When our ethical standard is raised in one facet of our lives, it will carry over to others. Such small changes will, ultimately, result in a *life-changing* character. By keeping a standard of honesty, and holding ourselves accountable to truth, we will behave in ways that are more responsible, respectable, and beneficial. We will be on time for the event so that we won't feel tempted to lie about our commitment to being punctual. We will be less stressed, as the burden of pristine memory (recalling the untruths and aligning stories) won't exist. We'll be less likely to act immorally toward friends, parents, children, and significant others. Affirming to oneself a moment-by-moment commitment to honesty will increase confidence, ultimately putting us in a position of admirable, justified influence.

Of course, this doesn't mean you should be callous, speaking your mind in every situation. Your commitment to honesty isn't a green light for being disrespectful or maliciously direct. Our commitment to truth needs to merge with a commitment to love—and love is not offensive. The book of Ephesians talks about how one should "speak the truth in love." So, when she asks if the dress makes her "look fat," you don't necessarily need to scream, "Hell yes!"

Maybe pray for a little divine discernment on that one …

Be Honest with Yourself

Think of the person who has lied to you the most in your lifetime. Was it a childhood friend, a parent, a sibling, a co-worker? Maybe even a current or former spouse? Let me take the liberty of answering the question for you. The person who has lied to you exponentially more than any other human is … you. That's right, if you identify the person who has deceived you the most as anyone other than the person you see in the mirror—*you're lying to yourself.* Russian novelist Fyodor Dostoevsky wrote, "Lying to ourselves is more deeply ingrained than lying to others." He's correct. It's more challenging to be truthful with our inner self than with any other person. After all, it's ourselves that we communicate with the most.

Just a few days after I began writing *It's a Process*, I was sitting at my cluttered desk reading *Man's Search for Meaning* by Viktor Frankl. My 10-year-old son barged into the room. He and I had returned from a long, tiresome baseball practice just a few minutes earlier, and—utterly exhausted—I was enjoying the downtime. In almost perfect irony, as my son excitedly asked me to go "play football" with him, I read these words:

> *Life ultimately means taking the responsibility to find the right answer to its problems and to fulfill the tasks which it constantly sets for each individual. These tasks, and therefore the meaning of life, differ from man to man, and from moment to moment.*

> —— *Man's Search for Meaning*, Viktor Frankl

I didn't want to get up. I wanted to read, study, and write. I also needed to spend more time polishing my resume, as I was still between jobs after being terminated from my supposedly "lifelong" career. However, I knew—at that exact moment—that I needed to define, at least in part, my own *meaning of life*. In my case, being a present, loving father trumped any project, any job, and just about any other responsibility. Up to that point in my life, I had often made the wrong decision when it came to what I was most dedicated to. Many of my problems had been the result of my own improper prioritizing. I was no stranger to the art of self-deception about what was important—and what was worth fighting for. But this time I wanted to get it right. I did not want to play football, but I did want to show my son how much I loved him; to let him know I cared, and to make it crystal clear to him that he was more important than a book. I immediately stood up and joined him in the backyard.

When we lie to ourselves about what really matters, we're seldom the only ones who pay the price. Sometimes those closest to us are the ones left loaded with the debt that we accumulated.

First, be honest with yourself. You'll then be better equipped to be truthful with others.

Grey Sausage

I remember when I first saw it: the large, glass baking dish my mom had just pulled from the oven. She had decided to branch out from her specialty cornbread and try her hand at weisswurst, a traditional Bavarian sausage that, I'm sure, was *supposed* to prove appetizing. However, I had a difficult time just getting passed the site of it. Covering the breadth of the pan were large, long sausages that I can only describe as … inappropriate. I felt like I was looking at a pile of "donkey dongs," as we'd put it in the stories we later told. With slight wrinkles, various shades of grey, and a firm texture, getting the nerve to put them near my face was a challenge. Nonetheless, I broke through my hesitation, cut off a large piece, and started chewing. That's when reality set in. It tasted worse than it looked. I forced myself to swallow, then stared down at my plate at what remained of the mule member. I couldn't do it.

My stepdad, Freddy, and my good friend Scott (who lived with us at the time) were fighting the same battle. They too were not impressed with the weisswurst. What were we to do? None of us wanted to confess to my mother our honest thoughts about the meal, which she had worked tirelessly to prepare. We had certainly been honest with ourselves about it, but not with the cook. Freddy had a plan.

He gestured to the "weisswurst willies" and declared, "You boys aren't allowed to eat anything else until you've eaten all of this. I don't care if it takes two weeks!"

For the next several days, Scott and I found ourselves having to sneak food from the pantry, lurking like ninjas in the shadows, searching for anything edible. We wanted nothing to do with the grey sausages and, eventually, they were simply too rotten to eat.

Now, this may not be the perfect example of how honesty should be applied in real-world situations. But I will say that, if we had mustered the courage to be upfront with my mom, maybe we could have avoided days of surviving as pantry pirates!

Social Support

One of the most effective ways to increase the chances of reaching a goal is to find social support. Retired Admiral William H. McRaven wrote, "You cannot paddle the boat alone." (McRaven 2017) Having a trusted associate can provide encouragement, accountability, and in some cases that forceful reprimanding that pushes one back on track.

We're creatures that thrive on social influence. Good friends make things easier. That said, it is vital that we welcome and embrace those who inspire a lifestyle of honesty. Be selective about friends. Just like how eagles don't fraternize with chickens, we must be extraordinarily careful about who we allow into our circle. Our divine destiny is too important to compromise with erroneous company, constantly hanging around those that embrace a life of deceit.

This may be easier said than done. Not everyone wants to take the narrow road, and that's okay. Many won't appreciate or respect perpetual honesty. In fact, some will resent it. You may find yourself more respected by a few, but you will also be begrudged. Much of the world is dependent on lies, and your commitment to truth will stir its demons. But this is part of making yourself better.

Paddle alone until God brings the right teammate into your life. It's better to move forward slowly than sink at the hands of a deceptive saboteur.

Father of Lies
A few years ago, I received a book in the mail called *Winning the War in Your Mind: Change Your Thinking, Change Your Life* by Pastor Craig Groeschel. I wasn't familiar with it and, at the time, had no idea who had it sent to me (thanks, mom). It turned out to be an excellent read, and a welcomed source of wisdom. There are several lines that stuck with me that I still embrace to this day.

"You cannot control what you do not confront." (Groeschel 2021)

This quote was big for me, as it resonated deeply with my personal experiences. Given the context of the book, I thought it was brilliant. However, I'd like to add my personal spin, a tail if you will: "You cannot control what you do not confront ... and you cannot confront what you don't know exists."

Unbeknownst to many, there is a dark, intangible force in our lives. Saul of Tarsus, later known as Paul (the Apostle), wrote a letter to his peers in the ancient Greek city of Ephesus. In it he writes:

> *For our struggle is not against flesh and blood, but against the rulers,*
> *against the authorities, against the powers of this dark world and against the spiritual forces of evil in the heavenly realms.*

—— Ephesians 6:12

It's scary, but it's true.

> *Your adversary is not your boss, spouse, child, ex, or neighbor with the demonic dog that is always barking. You may not realize it, but the one you are fighting against is your spiritual enemy, the devil.*
> *Sound too extreme?*
> *That's exactly what your enemy wants.*

— Craig Groeschel

This *does* sound extreme, too extreme for many. Which, as Pastor Groeschel noted, is the hope of that dark adversary.

But it is not enough to know he's there, lurking in the shadows of our lives. We need to know how he works—his tactics. It's one thing to fight a battle against an enemy you know nothing about. It becomes a very different encounter when you know exactly how the enemy operates.

When he lies, he speaks his native language, for he is a liar and the father of lies.

— John 8:44

In John's words, the devil is the "father of lies." This is no coincidence. When a person embraces a habit of deceit, it is because they are under the enemy's control—they are following *his* orders. Whether we are the victim of an untruth, or the assailant, Satan has the unrestrained power when lies are present. He has the upper hand. He's the *master* of deceit, the corrupt voice that warps our fear of uncertainty into the desire to be dishonest. He tricks us into believing we must use deceit to *avoid consequence, to build rapport, to garner wealth, to embellish, to trick, to manipulate, to get the girl or guy.* And his control often goes unrecognized: the tactic of a perfect stealth master.

What lies are you believing now? Do you sometimes feel like you have no purpose? Do you occasionally feel hopelessly lost in despair among an ocean of people who seem to "have it all"? Do you feel incapable of improving your physical health or appearance? Can't find the "right" job? Have you screwed up too many times? Is life simply too hard to carry on?

If any of these questions resonate, it's important to understand the source. *You've been manipulated into lying to yourself.* It may not seem that simple, but it is. As you move through *It's a Process*—and hopefully contemplate aspects of your own life—sincerely consider the lies you have believed that brought about struggle and heartache.

Subsequent chapters will dig deep into my journey of doing exactly that—an internal audit. I encourage you to join in and administer your own self-assessment. It starts with truthfulness with yourself. You've got to be real. It's *that* truth that is the effective foundation in our search to be better. We need to recognize and address our own faults, self-manipulations, and spiritual attacks.

We must *know* that lies are being fed to us at every moment but that, ultimately, we decide whether to adopt them.

Encouragement

John teaches us that "the truth will set you free" (John 8:32). Keeping a truthful heart will keep your path clear of obstacles that would otherwise inhibit your ability to live in peace. It will liberate you from the snares of the enemy, who will do all he can to trick you into feeling inadequate. That's why the commitment to verity must begin with a desire to be truthful with *yourself.* Don't allow lies about who or what you are to pervade your mind. You are strong; do not believe that you are weak. You are intelligent, capable, and gifted. To believe anything less is to trust a lie. Once we learn honesty with ourselves, we're prepared to be honest with others.

With a habit of truthfulness—toward both others and ourselves—our pursuit of betterment can prove fruitful. We can better align with God's intent for our lives when honesty is a nonnegotiable standard. Remember, God is truth. When we embrace honesty, we're in partnership with The Almighty.

Whether you're taking a young man hunting, living with a malicious deceiver, trying to avoid eating repulsive sausage, or just living everyday life, hold fast to the truth. Embrace honesty with the same commitment you do breathing. Doing so is the first step in living out our God-given purpose.

Everyone on the side of truth listens to me.

— John 18:38

IT'S A PROCESS

CHAPTER 2

COMPASSION

No act of kindness, no matter how small,
is ever wasted.

— Aesop

Rankin

Soon after my half-brother, John David, was born,
our small tribe of three finally moved off the Dorset
ranch and into one of the many run-down mobile
homes in the heart of Fort Davis. We were poor,
though I didn't know it. In fact, I would have argued
otherwise. I had escaped hell—and a kid blessed with
freedom and a rusted old Huffy bicycle is wealthy in
his own right. That next year I amassed dozens of
enduring memories: crawling through street gutters,
climbing the rocky butte that overlooked the town,
exploring abandoned buildings (illegally), and riding
every square inch of road I could find (most of which,
in the late 1980s, was still unpaved).

However, this would change in fifth grade when my
mother got a job as a teacher in another West Texas town.

Founded by a few bold ranchers in 1911, the small city of Rankin didn't gain traction until decades later, spurred by the region's insatiable lust for crude oil—"black gold" as locals sometimes call it. By the time we arrived in 1988, Rankin was a ghost of its former self. The main downtown street—once thriving with an eager, energetic population—could now hardly support its few remaining, struggling businesses. On the south side of town, beyond the railroad tracks, stood the derelict, three-story Yates Hotel that dominated what constituted Rankin's skyline. Laid to rest on the west side of town was the carcass of an old factory that had once been a proud exclamation of industry—but now the large letters reading "Halliburton" were a fading, barely legible whisper. On the southwest corner, the gutted remains of a once majestic movie theatre and, near it, a final definitive testament to the old town's past glory, the town gymnasium.

Just as in ancient Rome, stone images of various athletes adorned the main exterior wall: a football player, a basketball player, and a runner. My mother, brother, and I settled into our small house, directly across the street from these stone trophies. We were newcomers, unfamiliar nomads seeking refuge in a new, yet very old, community.

Basketball

A few years later, when I got to high school, my mother was married again, this time to a farmer named Freddy. He wasn't the most pleasant father figure and, combined with my relative immaturity, natural pessimism, and lackluster social skills, depression started to become a very real part of my character. Like a swing that is pushed away will find its way back, the feelings I had when living with Isaac began to return. I was eventually consumed by the darkness as life in Rankin continued around me.

Like so many West Texas towns, sports played an outsized role in the everyday life of Rankin High School. Everyone was expected to participate. I attempted the *big three*—football, basketball, and track. In football, I was simply too terrified to be effective. I let fear control me on the field. Track would eventually become a point of success for me, but not before I experienced Coach Booker's rage on the basketball court.

My brief career as a basketball player was interesting, to say the least. When it came to "hoops," my willingness to hustle was unmatched—but hustle isn't skill. I was sloppy and devastatingly uncoordinated, a "loping giraffe" as my teammates called me. My senior year, our coach, a loose-tempered man by the name of Ted Booker, was fiercely committed to winning at all costs. A *loping giraffe* like me would often ride the bench the entire game. Even if we had a 30-point lead, I would be twiddling the ol' opposables down to the last second. For a normal kid, this may not have been a big deal. But for a young man-child battling depression— along with holding a severe "I care what people think about me" complex—to suck at basketball meant sucking at life.

Every game felt like a dreadful eternity. I watched my teammates play, succeed, be praised, and glorified while I, a senior, sat alone—deemed too useless to contribute. My mental well-being, or lack thereof, grew very dark.

Before each game, Coach Booker gathered us together and had one of his star players lead the team in saying The Lord's Prayer. For most of the team (and coach), it was simply a tradition—a habitual regurgitation unworthy of sincerity. For me, however, it was a sacred moment. I would not join the others in reciting The Lord's Prayer, but instead, use that time very differently. While the team would mumble through the words from the Good Book, I would use those few seconds to offer my own prayer as fervently as possible. I would beg God, with all that I had, to kill me. Under my breath, I would desperately plead with Him to end my life. I meant it. At that moment, before I was scheduled to sit alone and witness others experience life, I wanted nothing more than death. I felt that was the only way out of the situation.

I had contemplated killing myself many times before but couldn't morally justify it. The thought of God willfully taking my life eliminated the confusing, difficult process of implementing a suicide. It was a dark, and unrelenting, existence. Like I said, to suck at basketball meant to suck at life.

Thankfully, God didn't end my life as I had asked. Instead, He did something very, very special.

Clark Fears Dean

Before the last home game of my senior year, I had sat on the bench for the entirety of 18 of our 21 games. My total playing time amassed was measured in seconds—not minutes—and this was a statistic not unnoticed by the many bullies (and girls) at school. On the popularity continuum, I was cemented on the unpleasant end. But something about my last game proved surprisingly different from those that had preceded it.

As I entered the gym for the last time as a Rankin basketball "player," the scene seemed denser, more energetic than the previous home games. I soon realized why. There were signs in the stands! Signs?! This was a 1A high school. People didn't bring signs—they were lucky to bring themselves, much less props to add flair to the proceedings. And then I read them: "Clark Fears Dean" sprawled across a white, flimsy banner. "Dean 3:16" screamed another. It appeared that some younger students, sophomores, had made signs for ME!

"Clark" referenced Trey Clark, a fierce competitor from the rival school, Irion County, who was known for his hellacious athletic ability. A few weeks prior we had heard rumors that he had shattered a backboard while dunking. In our district, he was a man among boys. "Dean 3:16" was a variant of "Austin 3:16," a term popularized by the famous wrestler Stone Cold Steve Austin. It seemed that I was either the butt of a cruel joke—or suddenly in style. In my pessimism, I assumed the former.

My Last Game
The game was electric. Fast, loud, and competitive—more so than usual. After sitting the majority of the game (as was the custom), and with only about seven minutes left, a chant from behind our bench rose.

"Noah! Noah! Noah!" the small group of students chanted. I was confused—unsure of what to think of the uncommon consideration. I leaned into my cynicism. Then another chant began to climb within the already energetic mob. "Put Noah in! Put Noah in! Put Noah in!" I couldn't help but smile, even while confident that the superficial "support" was meant to harm.

I looked to my left, across the bench toward Coach Booker. He was angry. No, he was pissed. He didn't hide his emotions well. He looked at the clock, then at the scoreboard. We were winning by 15 points with about 5 minutes left. Coach Booker ignored the chants, which began to subside. Then, with around 3 minutes remaining, still up by 15, the voices began rising again—but this time, with even more students joining the chorus.

"Noah! Noah! Noah!" they continued to a deafening crescendo. "Noah!!! Noah!!! Noah!!!" More had joined the mass—it was going viral. I looked down the bench at Coach Booker again. His jaws were locked, a fury on his face that I thought only a madman could harbor. "NOAH!!" he screamed. I sprang over to him.

He grabbed my jersey and pulled so violently that I almost fell into him. Rage was pouring from him. With a clenched fist, digging his knuckles into my chest, he forcefully spewed "DON'T EMBARRASS ME!" and shoved me onto the court. I ignored his fury.

When I took my first step onto the court, the stands erupted in a unanimous, ear-piercing cheer. Even those who didn't care suddenly did. The horde was all in with what a small group of sophomores had started. The gymnasium was more alive than I had ever witnessed. For the next few moments, I played as hard as I possibly could. No, I didn't score a point. No, I didn't make a good block or even steal the ball. Coach Booker was not impressed with my performance. But I gave it all I had right up to the buzzer.

Coley's Note

The next day at school, a few students joked with me about the experience. Although I had smiled through it all, in my soul, it hurt. I considered it a pity vote, a sad charade designed to entertain the masses.

While maneuvering from one class to another via the long school hallway, a young, blonde sophomore named Coley Johnson came toward me. As he approached, I recalled that he had been one of the students holding a sign the night before. Somewhat thin, with an athletic build, Coley wasn't the most popular kid in school, but he could have been. He was simply too humble for that role. When we connected, our eyes locked. He didn't say a word; he just handed me a small, folded piece of paper and continued down the hallway.

I opened it:

> Noah, I know that you sometimes feel depressed. I know that sometimes you feel hurt. But I want you to know that you have many friends who care about you. Those signs were for <u>you</u>. Those people were yelling for <u>you</u>. All of that was for you by people who care. You are not alone.

More than 30 years later, Coley's words are still singed deep in my memory. I'm thankful, not only for the encouragement that was so helpful to me at the time, but also the enduring reassurance from his act of kindness.

Compassion is awesome.

Compassion versus Indifference versus Animosity

What is Compassion?
One definition of compassion is "sympathetic pity and concern for the sufferings or misfortunes of others." Another suggests it's less about sympathy or pity, and more of a "motivation to alleviate suffering." In truth, compassion is an alloy of the two. It's *concern* followed by a *motivation* to alleviate. It is a recognition of suffering *combined* with an effort to ease the distress.

Compassion, in its truest form, involves a response—it is action based. Unfortunately, we're sorely lacking in compassion—as individuals, as communities, as a country, and as a world.

The Pendulum
Despair was prevalent throughout much of my life. For the longest time, I struggled with depression, unable to find joy. The Coleys of life were not abundant. However, it would be unfair to claim complete innocence on my part. Just because I've been disheartened does not mean I have been *good*. I've also failed to *be* a Coley. There are countless times that my

path crossed someone in need of compassion and I failed to act. In multiple instances, my own selfishness has revealed itself in the form of apathy for people I recognized to be suffering. Too often I've been provided an opportunity to help someone in need, and fallen short.

Even more shamefully, there are also instances in which I've been indescribably malicious. Although I claimed to follow the teachings of Jesus, my childish temper would sometimes reveal itself in the form of cruel outbursts. I'm not a violent person, but my lack of physical abuse didn't prevent me from wielding words as weapons. Unfortunately, I have caused far more destruction than a fist, knife, or bullet ever could. I've been the bully.

Like a pendulum, I have oscillated between kindness and malice. I've served as both predator and prey, healer and assailant. I've been labeled a "sweetheart," but also harbored a resentment that has revealed itself in vile forms.

Many people find themselves following a similar pattern. They, too, will be warm-hearted in one situation and bitter cold the next. The problem is, one temperament appears to be more promoted than the other. It seems we are encouraged to be less Coley... and more Isaac.

Media Influence

The Social Dilemma (2020) is a film that blends a documentary-esque vibe with a dramatic narrative to create one of the most terrifying films I've seen. It reveals, in incredible detail, how the very nature of social media cultivates addiction in the name of profitability—and its ability to influence people's opinions, emotions, and behavior. It also provides alarming insights into how social media impacts the mental health of adolescents, including its effect on the prevalence of teenage suicide. After watching the film, I became intrigued by our fascination and how the *bait* works so well. After doing a little investigation, I found a few interesting bits of information.

According to the Massachusetts Institute of Technology (MIT Initiative on the Digital Economy 2018), *false* news is approximately 70 percent more likely to be retweeted than accurate information. Further, accurate stories rarely reached more than 1,000 people, while the most prominent false-news items routinely reached between 1,000 and 100,000 people: "False news travels farther, faster, deeper and more broadly than the truth in every category of information—many times by an order of magnitude."

I don't care to delve into what constitutes *misinformation, disinformation, propaganda*, or whatever else. How information is classified doesn't matter. What does matter is how lies, of any kind, can transfer to us, and how we can be manipulated into accepting information that, in turn, causes us to believe something that is simply not true.

Does it really matter if we are slightly misinformed about whether Sylvester Stallone has rabies or if Mr. Rogers was a Navy SEAL? Perhaps not. But false information spreading exponentially faster than the truth isn't just about Mr. Stallone's health. It's often *emotionally stimulating* information that makes for the fastest-moving—and ultimately most widespread presence—in the social media space. Can you guess what topics are the most "emotionally stimulating"? It's the *lies* that divide people, the deceptions that breed animosity.

Republicans are (whatever)! Democrats are (blank)! Black lives matter! *All* lives matter!! *NO* lives matter!!! Police brutality! Racism! Discrimination! Gay marriage! LGBTQ! Christians! Atheists! The list goes on and on.

I appreciate free speech, and I believe Jesus does, too. But, He seems less concerned with whether or not a person has the right to share thoughts, but more interested in *what* is said.

> *I tell you, on the day of judgment people will give*
> *account for every careless word*
> *they speak, for by your words you will be justified,*
> *and by your words you will be condemned.*
>
> —— Jesus (Matthew 12:36)

This is where the problem *lies*. We're too quick to believe, and act on, falsehoods. Too often we allow the "careless words" of social media to herd us into social groups bathed in animosity. By letting ourselves be steered by social media, we become conditioned to anger and dissension. We are trained to feel resentment. Instead of looking to help others, we fault them. We find ourselves living in an ever-present, paranoid state of bitter anxiety that causes us to create lines between us and the ones we are called to love.

We are being conditioned to withhold *compassion*.

Biblical Review

The Good Samaritan

In the Gospel of Luke, we read about a moment where Jesus was elaborating on the "Law". In part of His teaching, Jesus instructed the listeners there to "Love your neighbor as yourself."(Luke 10:27) In response, someone in the crowd then asked, "Who is my neighbor?" In other words, Jesus was invited to explain who should be considered worthy of being cared for to the same degree in which the listeners cared for themselves.

> In reply Jesus said: "A man was going down from Jerusalem to Jericho, when he was attacked by robbers. They stripped him of his clothes, beat him and went away, leaving him half dead. A priest happened to be going down the same road, and when he saw the man, he passed by on the other side. So too, a Levite, when he came to the place and saw him, passed by on the other side. But a Samaritan, as he traveled, came where the man was; and when he saw him, he took pity on him. He went to him and bandaged his wounds, pouring on oil and wine. Then he put the man on his own donkey, brought him to an inn and took care of him. The next day he took out two denarii and gave them to the innkeeper. 'Look after him,' he said, 'and when I return, I will reimburse you for any extra expense you may have.'

> Which of these three do you think was a
> neighbor to the man who fell into the hands
> of robbers?"
> (Luke 10:25-36)

Jesus was a master of leading people to truth without force-feeding them. The man who qualified as a "neighbor" was the Samaritan. But Jesus does much more than tactfully guide us into recognizing the hero of the story. He reveals how, exactly, neighbors are called to treat one another.

We know that compassion isn't shown unless action is taken to alleviate the suffering of another. It is two parts—recognition and action. And what happens in the parable? It was the man who called himself to *action* that did the right thing. Pity, which the priest and the Levite who passed by must have felt, was not enough. It was the man who combined his recognition of anguish with action who proved to be the worthy man.

What's not explicit in the story, which would have been obvious to the crowd listening, is that the man who had been stripped and beaten was a Jew. At that time, culturally, Jews and Samaritans were bitter enemies—they hated and feared one another. Typically, when their paths crossed, slanderous comments would have been a mild outcome, while interactions between the two groups often turned violent. This cultural propensity, which the listeners knew well, adds even more chutzpah to the Samaritan's action.

By stopping to help the Jew, the Samaritan was breaking an unwritten law. He was helping the *enemy*, ignoring the social line in the sand, and alienating himself by showing kindness to a Jew. His act of compassion was more than casual sympathy—it was a risk. The road to Jericho, where the parable takes place, was saturated with thieves and evil men, no doubt a motivator for the priest and the Levite to hurry past the injured man. The Samaritan's compassion was more than an allocation of resources. It could have had deadly consequences.

Christ-like compassion is a refreshingly unique blend of empathy and kindness. It's looking at a person with only love and, perhaps, a recognition that we should act to help them. Those are big shoes to fill, and I'm afraid we're coming up a bit short.

As a society, we have perpetuated the creation of barriers between groups. In today's world, it's common to segregate people, offering or denying rights based on certain characteristics. For example, over the past 60 years, hundreds of millions of dollars in scholarships have been awarded to students of a *required* race, creed, color, national origin, or sexual orientation. This mantra is echoed within the thousands of organizations that have adopted programs to promote diversity, equity, and inclusion by creating positions to be held exclusively by people *of a* specific trait like *race, creed, color, national origin, or sexual orientation.*

But is this the right approach?

How Should We Distinguish?

There is neither Jew nor Greek, there is neither slave nor free, there is no male and female, for you are all one in Christ Jesus.

— Galatians 3:28

When Jesus is asked what defines a neighbor, He is being prompted to point out how we should make distinctions, where to draw the line between groups of people—to paint a clear delineation between those who have the right to compassion and those who do not. Did Jesus suggest that we carefully consider cultural differences? Did He say something like, this?

"Listen, guys, first you really need to contemplate if the person in need of help is part of some minority or majority group, or if they're rich or poor, or ponder sincerely on whether you have helped other people of a similar race, creed, color, national origin, or sexual orientation before. Because you don't want to give too much or too little help to one group."

No, He didn't. The neighbor was the one who needed compassion. No other delineations were drawn. This goes against so much of what we're taught today. We are told to resent certain groups. We're told to level the playing field, to give scholarships to those people but not these people, to give jobs to that group but not this group, to allow a parade for this cause but not that cause, to pay for this person's medical bills but not that person. We're told that this group is evil, and that group is corrupt.

Of course, the intent of many of these mandates is founded in the pursuit of justice, but we're doing it wrong. The programs designed to promote justice and equality seem to promote the very problem they are designed to eliminate. They have the reverse effect.

Jesus didn't draw lines—and neither should we. That is the foundation of Christ-like compassion. When we offer prejudice, we are failing.

> *Do nothing out of selfish ambition or vain conceit.*
> *Rather, in humility value others above yourselves, not*
> *looking to your own interests*
> *but each of you to the interests of the others.*
>
> —— Philippians 2:3-4

The Solution

More than Motivation

> *Wherever there is a human being, there is an*
> *opportunity for a kindness.*
>
> — Lucius Annaeus Seneca

We have all heard motivational speeches that teach us to be selective about who we allow into our lives. They tell us, with inspiring and profound conviction, that we should excise those who don't provide a genuine contribution to our aspirations. We're taught that if a person isn't helping us, we should distance ourselves—reject them.

In many ways, this is sound advice. It's a justified suggestion—to rid ourselves of negative and destructive influences. I often teach my own children how important it is that they surround themselves with *good* people. However, the subtleties of what is being insinuated by such proposals must be understood. The wisdom outlined in these popular, stimulating lectures might be slightly misleading. There is a fine line between cutting people out of our lives that aren't helping us, and pushing people out of our lives who we are called to help.

The enemy doesn't want you to know the difference. Remember, he's the father of lies. He wants you to— ignorantly—put yourself first, forsaking everyone else, including those God has deliberately put in your path. Satan is clever. He's often the one chanting that selfish dialog that suggests anyone not making way for our success must be surgically removed.

Recognizing those we are called to help is not always easy. Acting on that recognition is still more challenging.

Compassion is not always comfortable—and that's the point. In life, we default to selfishness. We fight to ensure that we are happy, valued, wealthy, recognized, accomplished, and loved. Derailing this dynamic on someone else's behalf, especially an adversary, takes Christ-like motivation. It requires a U-turn, a detour, an otherwise inconvenient change in trajectory. It takes *sacrifice*.

Compassion is Sacrifice

*And do not forget to do good and to share with others,
for with such sacrifices God is pleased.*

— Hebrews 13:16

Of the many lessons to be extracted from the parable of The Good Samaritan, one of the more resounding is that compassion takes conscientious effort. It requires offering valuable resources—time, energy, money, influence—that can sometimes feel bothersome or annoying.

Sacrificing a little of what we have is easier when we have plenty. It may be simpler still if all of our other needs are met and we're living a tranquil life. However, living in serenity is not necessary for charitable giving. Enjoying abundance isn't a requisite for generosity.

The Samaritan in the parable may have been wealthy, or he may have been poor. He may have been in a good mood or deeply agitated. He could have been the happiest man on earth or struggling with crippling depression. We do not know anything about his state of mind, financial condition, or relationship history because Jesus didn't tell us—and that's the point. It doesn't matter. We're called to sacrifice for the sake of others no matter what other conditions may be present, even if they don't do the same for us. We have a direct order to help others with no consideration for the extent to which they have reciprocated that generosity.

And there's a delightful paradox in that directive, a hidden gem in Jesus' parable. Both men, the Jew and the Samaritan, benefit from the charity.

Sacrifice and Purpose

Viktor Emil Frankl was born in March 1905 to Gabriel and Elsa Frankl in Vienna. As a teenager, Frankl had an extraordinary interest in psychology, so much so that he frequently corresponded with Sigmund Freud. He would eventually earn both his MD and PhD degrees from the University of Vienna, studying psychiatry and neurology. After achieving a smorgasbord of impressive academic achievements, Dr. Frankl joined Rothschild Hospital as the director of its Neurological Department in 1940. However, his tenure would be short-lived. Along with his wife and mother, he was soon transported by the Nazis to the Auschwitz-Birkenau concentration camp.

Though Dr. Frankl's mother and wife would both die at the hand of the Nazi regime, he survived the indescribable horror. In 1946, around a year after his liberation, he published *Ein Psychologe erlebt das Konzentrationslager* [A Psychologist Experiences the Concentration Camp], a book that was eventually titled *Man's Search for Meaning* by his American publisher. In this magnificent manuscript, Dr. Frankl details extraordinary stories of love, hate, good, evil, struggle, liberty, and more. He also offers an introduction to something he called "logotherapy," a therapeutic approach that guides people to find meaning in life. It's a form of psychotherapy that suggests that hardship (suffering) can lead to feeling a sense of *purpose*. In one particular passage, Dr. Frankl provides an example of how logotherapy is applied:

Let me cite a clear-cut example: Once, an elderly general practitioner consulted me because of his severe depression. He could not overcome the loss of his wife who had died two years before and whom he had loved above all else. Now, how could I help him? What should I tell him? Well, I refrained from telling him anything but instead confronted him with the question, "What would have happened, Doctor, if you had died first, and your wife would have had to survive you?" "Oh," he said, "for her this would have been terrible; how she would have suffered!" Whereupon I replied, "You see, Doctor, such a suffering has been spared her, and it was you who have spared her this suffering—to be sure, at the price that now you have to survive and mourn her." He said no word but shook my hand and calmly left my office. In some way, suffering ceases to be suffering at the moment it finds a meaning, such as the meaning of a sacrifice (Frankl 2006).

The patient in the story is forced to mourn the loss of his companion. Dr. Frankl himself had suffered the loss of his own wife, countless friends, and endured unimaginable grief in the concentration camps. Both men had experienced tremendous loss. But the premise of logotherapy holds true even in relatively minor situations. Going out of your way to help someone may not be legitimate "suffering" (relative

to the extremes outlined in *Man's Search for Meaning*)
but helping people, even in seemingly insignificant
forms, can yield a sense of purpose.

Every day we hustle through life in an effort to fulfill our
wants and desires. We zoom in on ourselves. We save money
to buy that one thing we think will bring us joy or find time
to do that activity we're certain will make us happy. However,
it's when we look to our periphery and act for the advantage
of others that we truly benefit ourselves. The key to
happiness is not buried under a new home, an inflated bank
account, or a robust investment portfolio. It is hidden in
other people. Sacrificing for the sake of others gives us a
sense of purpose like nothing else can. It's a wonderful
paradox that Jesus Himself revealed more than 2,000 years
ago.

Compassion equals life.

> *In everything I did, I showed you that by this kind of*
> *hard work we must help the weak, remembering the*
> *words the Lord Jesus himself said:*
> *'It is more blessed to give than to receive.'*

—— Acts 20:35

Be Different
In a world lacking compassion—a problem being exacerbated
by media influence—we should have the audacity to be
unique, fully prepared to help those in need, and remain
steadfast in that mission. With a perpetual willingness to
sacrifice on behalf of others, we will feel a lasting sense of

purpose—confident that our existence has meaning.

But how can we maintain such a noble effort? How can we "remain steadfast" in a mission to help others when our own inherent nature pulls us in the opposite direction? In a word, courage. We must be daring—fighting the urge to believe the lies we're being inundated with on a daily basis. Garnering unnecessary, superficial possessions won't elicit long-term contentment. Being accepted by that group or organization will not, on its own, yield enduring happiness. Political parties, designer clothes, and stylish (whatever) have nothing to do with our meaning and purpose. We must destroy the boundaries we have been taught to create and erase the lines in the sand that others have drawn for us. A person's race, creed, color, national origin, or sexual orientation doesn't matter. Anyone can be worthy of compassion. We must embrace a new way of thinking—a unique, uncommon mindset.

We are called to *be different.*

> *Do not be conformed to this world, but be transformed*
> *by the renewal of your mind, that by testing you may*
> *discern what is the will of God, what is good and*
> *acceptable and perfect.*

—— Romans 12:2

Encouragement

We have all had those moments when someone took the time to help us—to show genuine compassion. I encourage you to reflect on those moments—recall those blessings. Then consider the opportunities you've missed to do the same. When did you fail to be a Coley in someone's life? Do you remember a missed opportunity to show compassion? My challenge to you is to have fewer *missed* opportunities. Be the person who eases the suffering of another.

Although you may not see it, you do have what it takes to make someone else's life better—and in return help yourself. You have incredibly valuable resources that can bring life to all those involved. Can you sing? Then sing to those who enjoy song. Are you a CPA? Offer your services to those who struggle with taxes. Are you a carpenter or plumber? Agree to share your skills with those in need. Can you dance? Write? Run? Whatever it is, find a way to help people. Even if all you can do is take a flimsy poster board to a basketball game, or write an encouraging message on a small piece of paper. Do it.

That is Christ-like compassion.

Each of you should use whatever gift you have received to serve others, as faithful stewards of God's grace in its various forms.

— 1 Peter 4:10

IT'S A PROCESS

CHAPTER 3

WORK ETHIC

A man is worked upon by what he works on. He may carve out his circumstances, but his circumstances will carve him out as well.

—— Frederick Douglass

No Quitting

From the time I was very young, one characteristic my mother embedded within me was the concept of *work ethic*.

"You don't have to try it. But if you start, you can't quit."

That was my mom ... often.

This "it" was anything from sports to livestock shows to acting class to college. She was steadfast in her mission to not forge defeatists. Although I was never particularly gifted in any one domain, especially basketball, my willingness to work through adversity proved rewarding—more often than not. However, I eventually learned that there was a caveat to my mom's rule, a hidden loophole.

53

Developing a strong work ethic is important, but how it is applied is just as critical.

Throughout childhood and young adulthood, I had a relatively healthy relationship with effort. Unfortunately, such a mentality did not blend well with my failure to rationalize. I wasn't always the brightest crayon in the … knife drawer. Like a stubborn mule struggling to climb a steep, perilous mountainside—while not noticing the obvious walking path leading to the top—I was rarely willing to stop, slow down, and logically think through how to work toward a particular goal. I would skip contemplation; all gas, no brakes. Inefficiency became my unspoken mantra.

Still, one good thing about being willing to work harder than most everyone else—even if combined with stupidity— was that it was relatively simple to succeed in activities that required effort alone. Track was one such endeavor. You don't have to be smart to run hard.

Think Forrest Gump.

Touching the Fence Post

Track is the purest form of sport. You say,
"We're going to see who can get from here to there the
fastest." That's it.

— Coach Gabe (~2001)

I was willing to put in the work—to hurt. In middle and

high school, when others would lie about completing the running workout assigned to them, I would run *all the way*—to the cemetery, light tower, or whatever random landmark coach picked out that day. When he said to run 8 x 400s, I would run *all* of them while others would skip as many as they could get away with. This mentality would, eventually, lead me to a full scholarship at Angelo State University in Texas.

I remember one particular incident during my time there, on a blistering fall day when my teammate Jerry and I were instructed to run "ten sprints from the tree to the tennis court". Our coach, James Reid, would not oversee the work, as he trusted us both to give a valiant effort without being micromanaged. Jerry looked like a typical runner—average height, lean build, and to the ignorant eye, nothing particularly unique. But in the three years I had known him, I had witnessed the transition this unassuming man could make. I had seen Jerry kick through a pickup windshield, knock a fraternity guy unconscious, and rip apart a steel gate with his bare hands—a typical weekend. On the track, he was an athlete. Off of it, Jerry was a violent hellraiser who was not to be trifled with.

We began our walk toward the dry, dead-grass hill as Coach Reid had instructed.

"Ready, go!" I said as I darted up the slope toward the tennis court fence. It wasn't all that far, but a sincere effort to sprint made it challenging. I hustled all the way to the fence and touched the pole next to the court, before turning around to slowly jog back down to the tree for a second run. Jerry had turned around early—he hadn't touched the tennis court pole. Typically, I was not one to correct, counsel, or coach. Even today, I'm very much a "live and let live" person, not interfering with someone if they choose to ... whatever. However, I considered Jerry a friend and wanted the best for him. I knew that he had the ability to do the job right, but he just didn't have the right mindset; his work *ethic* didn't match his work *capacity*. I respected him enough to call him out ... delicately.

"Jerry," I said, in the least aggressive way possible. "Listen, man. I'm not trying to tell you what to do. I'm not your coach. You're a good athlete, so just touch the court post. It's not going to be that much harder to run that little bit at the end—but it will make you better. C'mon, man. You got this."

Usually, Jerry was not one to comply. But he knew I was sincere—he knew I was right. He stood silently, looking down at the ground. The rage that I had so often seen him unleash on others was roiling within himself. He was battling his own resolve. After a moment, Jerry nodded in agreement. On our next sprint, he ran all the way to the tennis court post. His work ethic had been upgraded.

Understanding Work Ethic

Work Ethic

Work ethic can be defined as *the principle that hard work is intrinsically virtuous or worthy of reward*. It can also be *a great deal of effort or endurance*. By merging the two, we can describe work ethic as *the principle that, offering a great deal of effort or endurance is intrinsically virtuous or worthy of reward.* In other words, having a "good work ethic" is believing (and acting on) the idea that committing to the work is worth it. But what exactly is this "reward"?

The ambiguity of what constitutes adequate "reward" illuminates the countless miscalculations and misinterpretations humans have made when it comes to work. People have, sometimes for their entire lives, put forth a "great deal of effort," only to find the reward sorely lacking. The problem is one of allocation. It's where, precisely, this *work ethic* is directed. Is the work being done going to result in the desired reward? Is the reward going to elicit the sense of accomplishment that one hopes? The truth is, many times the unexpected answer to at least one of these questions turns out to be "no." We often unwittingly misallocate our hard work, mismanage our *great deal of effort or endurance*, and all we are left with is regret.

Soon after my wife and I moved to College Station, I found myself dedicated purely toward two things: my studies and my aesthetics. I would go to school during the day and hit the gym in the evenings. My wife, whom I had made a covenant with to prioritize above all other worldly pursuits, was not my top priority. Sure, we would spend time together, going out to eat or periodically catching the latest flick at the local movie theater, but not before I had taken care of my "top two." Thankfully, that season of immense selfishness passed, but my tendency to miss the mark with my prioritization choices did not.

Later in life, when our two children were young, I would

find myself torn between a myriad of responsibilities: juggling a full-time job, running two small companies, working as a CrossFit emcee, going to the gym, serving as a husband, being a present father, and trying to squeeze in a bit of rest. Being a father and husband were certainly among my priorities, but I'm not certain that they were my primary concerns. I was so focused on achieving what I believed was success that I was failing my family. Even though the two businesses I ran were headquartered in a barn just a few yards from our home, I would fail to de-emphasize certain aspects of life and make what was most important *actually* most important. I was too focused on some things, and not focused enough on others. The root of my miscalculation was my commitment to pursuing the wrong rewards. I was a zombie—an ignorant, undead corpse hell-bent on garnering money and prestige. Although I was working harder than anyone I knew, I was getting no closer to true success. I had a great work ethic but was mismanaging my effort. Thankfully, I finally found a balance.

Depending on your role, making money may be a key obligation. For me, being the breadwinner is a crucial responsibility. If I ignored the mortgage payment, electric bill, or funds needed for groceries, I would be failing. However, I would also be failing if I did not embrace time with my family, including real vacations where I put work aside. Without balance, a collapse of some kind is inevitable. When all our eggs are in one basket, a sacrifice is made, and loss occurs.

This happens to all of us, to some degree or another.

Success

How do you define "success"?

Most definitions of *success* involve something like money, fame, wealth, affluence, etc. In the book *The Formula: The Universal Laws of Success*, author Albert-László Barabási hints as to how he defines success: "…we can't rely on sheer instinct, strong performance, or all the old inspirational clichés if we want our work to be appreciated, our accomplishments to be noticed, and our legacies to endure." (Barabási 2018, 12) He goes on to be more explicit by suggesting that success is, "the rewards we earn from the communities we belong to." (Barabási 2018, 12) It seems, according Barabási, achievement is closely tied to influence—it is our impact that defines achievement. It is all about "reward".

Many people fail to see the proper context in which this definition should apply. Although it could be taken in the appropriate framework, many miss the mark. They are convinced that our ultimate purpose, the slate on which we compare our value and worth, is in the hands of others—how people rank us. Many believe their definitive triumph is the extent to which people appreciate them, notice their accomplishments, and capture their legacy. This misconstrued perspective occurs because we have convinced ourselves that having more than "the other guy" will bring us to a state of elation. It is this mentality that serves as the crux for the imbalance—when too many eggs get tossed into that single basket.

The truth is, many visions of grandeur—wealth, fame, and/or financial prosperity—can be worth pursuing, but it is not the only way to get to "success"… and it certainly isn't for everybody. We all need to pay the bills. But we are not called to crave unnecessary fortunes.

Hard Workers of the World

Heath Ledger, the famous actor, started acting at ten years old. As his career blossomed, he developed a reputation for holding a hardened, uncommonly strong work ethic. In preparation for what would prove one of his most iconic roles (the Joker in *The Dark Knight*), Ledger locked himself in a hotel room to perfect the complex character's voice and mannerisms. If you've seen the film, you know how masterfully he performed. Elizabeth Taylor began young as well, first acting at age nine and ultimately starring in dozens of movies, including her acclaimed performances in blockbuster juggernauts such as *Giant* (1956) and *Cleopatra* (1963). Later in life, she became a prominent HIV/AIDS activist, and the first woman to create and market her own line of fragrances—from which she boasted two best-selling perfumes. Carlos Ghosn, the former chairman and CEO of Nissan, flew more than 150,000 miles per year for business purposes and was described in *Forbes* as the "hardest-working man in the brutally competitive global car business." (Muller 2006) Dennis Rodman, the colorful bad boy of the 1990s, played professional basketball for twenty-one years, amassing five championships, eight All-Defensive team honors, two All-Star recognitions, and a cascade of other accolades. At the peak of his career, Rodman had a net worth of over $26 million.

These people all had an uncommon work ethic. They all displayed a great deal of effort and were heavily rewarded for it. Their work has been appreciated, their accomplishments noticed, and their legacies have certainly endured. By definition, they are resoundingly successful.

Let's take a closer look.

Heath Ledger was so stressed that he couldn't sleep. His perpetual anxiety, set ablaze by his desire to perfect his roles, left him unable to relax. "I couldn't stop thinking. My body was exhausted, and my mind was still going," Ledger once said (Lyall 2007). He died on January 22, 2008, with six different medications in his blood, including oxycodone, hydrocodone, and diazepam. Elizabeth Taylor married eight times, became a blistering alcoholic, and developed a crippling addiction to painkillers. Carlos Ghosn, at the time of writing, lives as an international fugitive in Lebanon, with charges of breach of trust, misuse of company assets for personal gain, violating multiple securities laws, and a laundry list of other no-nos. Dennis Rodman, while being inducted into the NBA Hall of Fame, was given the opportunity to speak boldly about his *success* as a professional basketball player. Onstage, he revealed the one, single regret of his illustrious career. Through soft sobs Rodman uttered, "I wish I had been a better father." (OfficialHoophall 2012)

The most successful people in the world can concurrently be colossal failures.

The Trade-Off

Just because someone has financial wealth, worldwide recognition, or NBA stardom doesn't mean they've built a collection of collapsed relationships, moral degradation, or a criminal history. However, often the determination, drive, and laser-like focus to "succeed" distracts from other forms of success. An unbridled commitment to winning in one area may lead to failure in another. Goals must be managed, prioritized. This is where discernment comes in. This is where the *reward* must be defined. This is how work ethic … works.

While studying Kinesiology, I learned extensively about a phenomenon called the Speed-Accuracy Trade-Off. It references the tendency of the accuracy of a specific task to diminish the faster one moves. In other words, the faster you go, the less accurate you tend to be. See the simple test below as an example of how the trade-off works.

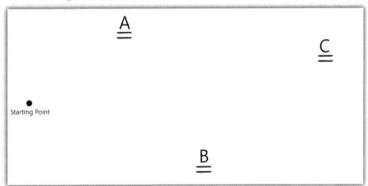

Recreate the image above on a sheet of paper. Start by putting your pen on the "Starting Point." The objective is to draw a line from the Starting Point between the two parallel lines marked "A," then between the two lines marked "B," and finishing through the lines marked "C." Notice that, in general, the faster you try to complete the task, the more difficult (less accurate) it becomes. This is the "Speed/Accuracy Trade-Off."

Regarding this rudimentary example, "success" was accomplished by drawing a line between each set of parallel lines. If the line drawn did not pass between the two target lines, the attempt was a failure no matter how slow or fast it was drawn. Similarly, in our everyday lives, we have many options for how to direct our efforts—how *fast* we want to accomplish our goals. Sure, we can prioritize garnering gratitude and prestige from the communities to which we belong. But make no mistake, more often than not, such hyper-focused effort can result in failure in other arenas of life. There will be a trade-off.

This is why the term "success" cannot have a universal definition. This is why the description by Albert-László Barabási stating "the rewards we earn from the communities we belong to" needs to be carefully pondered. The *rewards* should be judiciously defined. The ideal "communities" probably aren't untold numbers of strangers set to admire one's wealth, fame, prestige, accomplishments, or entrepreneurship prowess. Instead, we need to consider our primary audience to be those closest to us—those who really matter; like a husband, wife, son, daughter, and friends. Rushing through life to become "successful" at something that doesn't really matter may cost the relationships with those who do.

Workaholics

*Like cocaine, work is extremely addictive, but unlike
drug addictions, overwork has society's blessing.*

— Barbara Killinger

Work is a good thing—it is necessary and essential.
Being productive excites us. It can develop our strengths,
contribute to our well-being, and offer a sense of
accomplishment. Work helps us to build confidence, provide
a healthy intellectual challenge, foster the learning of valuable
skills, and stimulate a better understanding of life in general.
Of course, work can offer financial rewards, too, which can
ease burdens. Labor can be terrific.

But, there is a limit. Sometimes we take it too far.

Workaholism is an obsessive, neurotic, desire to do more
and more. And it's very much an addiction. According to the
late Dr. Barbara Killinger, "a workaholic is a person who
gradually becomes emotionally crippled and addicted to
control and power in a compulsive drive to gain approval and
success" (Killinger 1991, 6). The obsession with work stems
from a competitive, ego-driven, perfectionist personality.
Once the *reward* from applying that behavior is realized, there
comes an adrenaline high that hooks the workaholic—and
the spiral begins. More work equals more reward, and, like a
cocaine addict, a preoccupation consumes the user. He/she
becomes compulsive. The need for a fix is the driving force
behind the endless efforts. Labor then becomes
unrecognizably troublesome.

Workaholics define themselves—their sense of purpose—by their work. Like most addicts, they are blind to the truth of their dependence. And there's a deep, dark trap awaiting them. They become chained to the traits that characterize their dilemma: obsessive, narcissistic, selfish, controlling, and paranoid. The price of worldly pursuits comes at the cost of their very character. Pastor and theologian Timothy Keller noted "When work is your identity, success goes to your head, and failure goes to your heart." (Keller 2014)

There are severe consequences to not finding a balance between working to live and living to work. Without intervention, the workaholic is doomed—and the effects of workaholism are felt by more than just the addicted. Others can suffer collateral damage, and in many cases, these "others" feel the effects even more than the workaholic.

Sam
"I blew it." (McCahill 2013)

Those were the last words of Sam Walton, the founder of the colossal corporate entity known as Walmart. His bones brittle with cancer and his blood defeated by leukemia, one of the most respected entrepreneurs of all time lay in a hospital bed in Little Rock, Arkansas. At the time, his holding company employed 380,000 people and experienced annual sales of almost $50 billion. He alone was worth around $8.6 billion (Celebrity Net Worth n.d.). Walton had been widely praised by society, and many communities had shown him immense appreciation. However, none of that mattered in that hospital bed. Moments before his death, he would look up at his family—those he had neglected in order to build an empire—and be confronted with what I can only imagine was an eerily profound epiphany: it wasn't worth it.

Don't be like Sam.

Working Toward Neglect

Too often, a parent becomes obsessed with a particular goal, one that distances him/her from committing to being present. Under the guise that the work is for their betterment, workaholism can sever an otherwise healthy relationship with a son or daughter. The workaholic claims that they are working *for* the children—while perpetually abandoning them.

The plethora of empirical evidence revealing the catastrophic effects of (unnecessary) disregard is alarming. Neglecting children, especially for a prolonged period, can cause a variety of psychological and physiological problems. Mental disorders, substance abuse, suicide attempts, learning disabilities, sexual promiscuity, post-traumatic stress disorder (PTSD), and an increased likelihood of violent behavior are all potential repercussions for children who are continually neglected. And the list goes on. Data revealing the horrendous effects of child neglect is seemingly unending.

However, there are far too many parents who don't realize that they are failing. They're putting too much effort on speed, not accuracy—moving fast, working hard to succeed, but ignoring those that need attention. They are not keeping their priorities *between the lines*, a tendency that can be passed on.

Workaholism, like many addictions, can transfer to children. Just like alcohol and drug abuse by a parent will increase the likelihood of a child adopting such inhibiting addictions, the preoccupation with work will increase the odds that a child develops an obsessive, neurotic, desire to do more.

> *Growing up in a dysfunctional family guided by such rules, children learn to value themselves according to what they do, how well they perform, and what tasks or goals they accomplish. Children are not valued or accepted for how they are,*
> *separate from what they do.*

— Barbara Killinger

Of course, the collateral damage of workaholism expands beyond children.

Marital Breakdown
Research done by Dr. Bryan E. Robinson the University of North Carolina at Charlotte found that "the divorce rate among workaholics is 40 percent higher than the rest of the population." (Reeves 2005) And such is no surprise.

Like a parasitic leech, the destructive preoccupation with one's career travels with the host. The workaholic will be thinking about work even during intimacy (in the relatively few moments they find the time to do so). When on vacation, a workaholic's obsession will follow him or her. Quality time with a significant other becomes less and less of a priority, and the relationship plateaus, suffering in multiple ways.

I met a man once, I'll call him Gerald, who was very successful financially. In a room full of young, hard-working men aspiring to be equally accomplished, he spoke proudly of all he had achieved. The lake house, the ranch, the vacations—and especially his new, shiny Corvette—were all points of pride. Gerald laughed as he boasted about how fast the car was, how clean the interior was, and even how he had taken it turkey hunting for some crazy reason. But then something happened with Gerald, *within* him. Just as a movie changes scenes, his thoughts shifted and his smile vanished. He grew quiet, and the sea of young onlookers—I, one of them—matched his silence. His enthusiasm had been shattered, and an odd silence blanketed the room. He looked down and softly spoke.

"I gave up my wife for this."

Suddenly, he was drowning in regret.

There are times when we need to stop and look around, to catch a glimpse of our situation. We can become so hyper-focused, our attention and effort so singularly allocated, that we can't see what's around us. Sometimes we need to take a rest from the rat race to recognize the maze we're in.

We won't be able to see our divine purpose if we do not look *up*.

Biblical Review

Work to Live

Work is not wrong or bad. In fact, it's divinely inspired. God Himself was the first worker in existence!

In the beginning
God <u>created</u> the heavens and the earth.

—— Genesis 1:1

This simple, short sentence teaches us that God, at least in part, is a worker. Considering we are made in His image (Genesis 1:27), it is no surprise that we too have an inherent inclination to work. The need to "create" is a fire that burns within the core of every person. That's why we experience that sprinkle of elation after we have successfully completed a task. And what a gift this is! Our God-given nature to work can yield immeasurable benefits and is of paramount importance to our lives.

The Book of Psalms mentions that each of us "will eat the fruit of [our] labor" (Psalm 128:2). Much like animals, our very survival depends on our commitment to work. The words from Paul's second letter to his friends in the ancient city of Thessalonica echo this.

For even when we were with you, we gave you this rule:
'The one who is unwilling to work shall not eat.'

—— 2 Thessalonians 3:10

However, work is not just a rudimentary hunter-gatherer tool to keep us alive. We are called to labor for more than just ourselves. Our God-given need for productivity has been put in place for the benefit of others as well.

Work to Love

In Paul's first letter to his friend and apprentice, Timothy, he wrote:

> *Anyone who does not provide for their relatives, and especially for their own household, has denied the faith and is worse than an unbeliever.*

—— 1 Timothy 5:8

God takes work seriously. A person who denies work cannot follow their divine path. But this does not mean our goal should be amassing loads of financial wealth. Despite what the world, and a tax-hungry government, would have us believe, money has very little to do with *real* purpose. It took me decades to fully appreciate this principle, to de-emphasize wealth accumulation as the supreme objective of my existence.

We should work, not just for our own well-being, but for the benefit of those around us. We should strive to mirror the God-like trait of labor to show our love and commitment to family, friends, and even strangers. This is very similar to the concept of offering compassion to others outlined in Chapter 2. The money we make is just a tool for accomplishment of this divine directive. You don't need extravagant wealth to *sacrifice* for the sake of others.

The Work Only You Can Do

*You are the light of the world. A city set on a hill
cannot be hidden. Nor do people light a lamp and put
it under a basket, but on a stand, and it gives light to
all in the house. In the same way, let your light shine
before others, so that they may see your good works
and give glory to your Father who is in heaven.*

—— Matthew 5:14-16

In the summer of 2022, my fourteen-year-old daughter,
McKinlee, returned home from a five-day church camp.
When I inquired about her time there, her response was
profound. She revealed that her experience was exponentially
more than pointless games and adolescent activities—that I
had assumed would sum up her involvement. She mentioned
Paul's first letter to his church allies in Corinth, where he
references the "Body of Christ." Although I was vaguely
familiar with the passage, it was McKinlee who exposed the
powerful lesson, the treasure of wisdom so few seem to
uncover.

*Now you are the body of Christ, and each one of you
is a part of it.*

—— 1 Corinthians 12:27

For years, I had been defeated by my tendency to
compare my own accomplishments against those of others.
McKinlee pointed out that, by making these contrasts, I was
directing myself away from the path best suited for me. She

71

taught me, through scripture, that each of us has a distinct role in this world. Instead of separating ourselves through comparison, we're called to consider ourselves as different parts of one body.

> *Some of us are lungs, some of us are the heart, some of us are hair, some are eyes, etc.*
>
> — *McKinlee Dean*

Our purpose may be *similar* to others, but make no mistake, no one on earth has the exact same divine purpose. Again, we're not all called to be butterflies.

Through her simple yet profound analogy, McKinlee made me realize that I needed to adopt a new perspective, one that would guide my work not at goals that I had created based on comparison, but toward objectives that God had outlined for me. Our real purpose, the direction of our effort—the lines that we need to be moving through—is person-specific. If we don't welcome this truth, we could find ourselves at the end of our lives with a heart-breaking epiphany. We've done it all wrong.

The Solution

We Can Miss It

In each person's life, careful assessments must continually be made. We must consider intently what really matters. Each time an unbiased review is made, priorities will reveal themselves. It is our duty to then ensure that our efforts are being leveled in that direction. And despite what motivational memes suggest, there can come a point when it's too late to course correct. Although a person always has purpose in life, one can miss a God-given calling—a sad truth that some can't accept. Some people will justify even their most foolish decisions by claiming "everything happens for a reason." The truth is, everything *does* happen for a reason, and sometimes that reason is foolish men making foolish decisions. I know, because I've been that guy!

Thankfully, God is more patient than we deserve. He has mercy that is beyond our comprehension. That's why it's called *amazing* grace. Like the navigation app on your smartphone, God doesn't get upset, frustrated, or malicious when we veer off course. We are simply nudged to "reroute" when we've made a wrong turn stemming from prioritizing our own selfish ambitions. But we must listen. Turning off the directions app and expecting to end up in the right destination doesn't make much sense.

Make the Change

If you are a workaholic, start taking steps to break that addiction. You were not designed to be a slave to anything, even a socially acceptable compulsion like work. If you find yourself neglecting your spouse, children, and friends to pursue "success," you are headed in the wrong direction. It's time to course correct. The size of our home, the level of our bank account, and the number of our social media followers do not define our value. The extent to which our legacies are appreciated and noticed by others won't prove worthwhile if we have compromised our God-given calling.

Eulogy

*So I hated life, because the work that is done under
the sun was grievous to me.
All of it is meaningless, a chasing after the wind.*

— Ecclesiastes 2:17

The author of Ecclesiastes may seem like a bitter, old pessimist. However, the words of this wisdom book are dripping with truth. The point being made is not that our work cannot have value. It's that if we fail to understand the purpose of our work, we're indeed wasting our efforts. If our sole purpose—our meaning of life—is found in something as insipid as an occupation, we are headed for a colossal disappointment. To *toil under the sun* out of an envious urge to build wealth, garner praise, and gain power is, ultimately, "meaningless." We need to understand that *chasing after the wind* is an endless effort. Our work must mean more; it must be *for* more.

Imagine yourself at your funeral. Picture yourself standing at the back of the room, with your clean, shiny casket centered at the front. When the solemn service begins, one by one, various family members and friends stand to speak. What do you want them to say? In your mind, what's the perfect way for others to show tribute to your contributions? What, exactly, would you want your son or daughter, brother or sister, mother or father, or closest friends to say?

I would want my children to give examples of how I was always willing to stop whatever I was doing to spend time with them. I would want them to confidently boast that I was a loving, supportive, complimentary, patient, guiding, and most importantly, present father. I would want my wife to feel that I was faithful, loving, and supportive. I have learned, however, this cannot happen if my idea of having a work ethic is making the most money I can, no matter the cost (pun intended).

This eulogy scenario helps me to better understand how to make everyday decisions. It helps me distance myself from the envy that would otherwise drive me to work hard, earn extra, and buy more stuff than the other guy. It helps me align my actions with what really matters. I encourage you to play out this scenario in your own mind often. You may find yourself taking roads less traveled—those based on *purpose*.

Encouragement

Think carefully about your life, your relationships, and where you apply your work ethic. What have you been over-prioritizing? Who or what have you been neglecting?

It can seem daunting to challenge the rest of the world (and yourself) by going against what has been engrained within us to prioritize. It's not always easy to "lean not on [our] own understanding" (Proverbs 3:5) when we are inundated with a monsoon of propaganda telling us that success is directly tied to how much power, fame, and fortune we have. Change isn't always easy… but it may be necessary.

My encouragement to you is this. You have a specific, God-ordained purpose. You have duties, responsibilities, even deadlines, all carefully forged in a divine blueprint that, believe it or not, will lead you to your most fulfilled life. It may be a calling of financial wealth or it may be a vocation of humble poverty. It may be a path that leads to worldwide notoriety or to anonymity. Your legacy may endure for thousands of years—or die with you. But make no mistake, the only way to fail is to work toward the goals not outlined for you by God. Yes, it will take a hardened, focused work ethic to follow that blueprint, but you have what it takes. You just need your work ethic to match your work capacity. Use sincere prayer to guide you—to help you discern how, where, or to whom to apply that work ethic. And whatever it is, do it right.

Touch the tennis court post—and let God orchestrate the rest.

CHAPTER 4

SELF-ESTEEM

---

*The worst loneliness is to not be
comfortable with yourself.*

— Mark Twain

Getting Out of the Blocks ... Or Not

"On your marks!"

I cautiously stepped forward and settled into the tattered blocks. I looked down at the faded white mark that denoted the starting line—my thumbs and index fingers set methodically against its edge, hands spread apart a little wider than my shoulders. The surface of the track was worn but not ragged. This was my first collegiate race, lane five. I couldn't think. My heart sprinted as if we were already running. Too many thoughts swarmed my mind; anxiety, excitement, fear, curiosity, dread, and hope poured through me like fire and ice. I was seconds away from the gunshot that would initiate my first attempt to run the 400-meter hurdles.

"SET!" the gunman announced, raising his arm toward the sky.

I locked my arms and pushed my legs into the starting position, forcing my butt upward. I had no idea what to expect. Time froze. I thought about the strange, awkward circumstances that had brought me to this point. I smiled at the irony of it all.

"BANG!"

I forced all the energy I could muster into my long, thin legs. It was game time … or so I thought.

The blocks slipped. Instead of me lurching forward like the other runners, I collapsed onto my chest, slamming into the faded starting line that I was so focused on only moments earlier. The piece of iron meant to serve as my springboard hadn't held—but there was no time to complain. The race had started; I was already in last place. I launched off the ground as best I could. Now, the chase.

As I ran, the hurdles that had seemed so intimidating during the weeks of training before came and went in the blink of an eye. It didn't feel like I was jumping over anything; instead, I was sprinting *through* them. As I got closer to the 200-meter mark—"halfway" I thought—but there was still plenty of work to do, and I had to stay attentive. Each hurdle demanded a laser-like focus, and the other runners seemed to be screaming for attention that I wouldn't give them. I was concentrating on *my* race. But then, as we came out of the last curve, something happened. Like the parting of the Red Sea, the other athletes disappeared from my peripheral vision—gone from existence. Before me was a long, straight path to the finish line—and only two hurdles to go. I couldn't hear anything, only the thought of what I *must* have done wrong. Did I skip a hurdle? Did everyone else stop for some reason? Something wasn't right. I was tempted to slow down and wait for the collapse of my magnificent illusion. But it didn't collapse—it was no illusion.

I would win the 400-meter hurdles.

The Transformation

Ultimately, it was that first race that proved the beginning of the end of my struggle with depression. The victory sparked something within me, a flicker of self-esteem that gave me the confidence to work harder, to believe I was *worth* it, and ultimately to learn something invaluable—the power of self-esteem.

And it all happened by chance.

After high school, I was adamant that I wanted to continue to be part of something. The various extracurricular activities I had participated in—except for basketball—had fostered a deep appreciation for social interaction. Friends were a comfort, and what better place to find friends than on a team?! But there was a big difference between the small fraternity at Rankin High School and the college campus of Angelo State University. One was a modest, 1A school that begged for participants, the other was one of the most admired Division II universities in the nation. In Rankin, I was a small fish in a small pond. Now, I was an amoeba in the ocean.

I didn't have a scholarship of any kind, but track was the only thing I thought I could survive. I decided to walk on … as a javelin thrower.

My first year at Angelo State University, I was six feet tall and weighed less than 150 pounds, a life-sized toothpick. I have no idea why, but the revered head coach David Noble entertained my presence on the team as a thrower—perhaps out of pity. My throws, if they could be called such, were so poor, so far below average, that I couldn't reach the "minimum mark." This means that my attempts were disregarded and literally not worth measuring. It was a laughable endeavor, to the point that, years later, I would be referenced as "quite possibly the worst javelin thrower in the history of the program" in *Track & Field News* (Bloomquist 2007).

That next year I faced my fears and walked on as a *runner*. It was that decision that, ultimately, put me in that less-than-perfect set of blocks. Winning my first collegiate race would initiate a multi-year transformation in which my character would gradually mutate from timidity and crippling self-doubt to boldness and blaring confidence. Ultimately, I would go on to earn a full scholarship, win a total of seventeen collegiate races, become a three-time All-American, and even be offered the opportunity to train for the 2004 Olympics. My boost in self-esteem transferred to life off the track as well. I eventually embraced academics seriously enough to move from a marginal 2.6 GPA in my undergraduate studies to earning a doctoral degree from Texas A&M University. However, my success as a collegiate athlete and academic paled in comparison to the real trophy I found in those years, which took the form of my beautiful wife, Lauren. The confidence I developed through track had given me the mojo to pursue the most beautiful woman I had ever seen—and it worked.

That first race changed everything for me.

Esteem: Sufficient or Inadequate?

Self-Esteem versus Self-Confidence

Self-esteem is the degree to which we *value* ourselves. Self-confidence, which slightly differs, is the level of trust a person has in his/her own ability, the degree to which one believes they are capable. Self-esteem references the perception of *value*; self-confidence references the perception of *competence*. Too little of either is detrimental—in many ways.

For years I was stuck in the abyss of depression with no esteem or confidence to speak of. From adolescence to my early college years, that void resulted in countless missed opportunities, unnecessary heartache, and an unjustified pessimism.

Pulled Out of the Pit

For some reason, my own insecurity caused me to view others as monstrously superior, fiendishly arrogant, or both. As such, I would often be hesitant to interact with strangers. Later in life, these feelings would turn into an unwarranted resentment for people I didn't know, which proved to be one of the most detrimental consequences of my lack of self-esteem. My own distorted view of myself caused me to create a warped view of others. Hot girls were sluts, athletic guys were jerks, rich people were spoiled, fat people were lazy, etc. I was a walking, talking beacon of inaccurate conviction. My own perceived lack of self-worth eventually translated into my becoming a judgmental, miserable hypocrite. This, of course, isn't conducive to making many friends. I would oscillate between depression, social isolation, and general disdain for others. But that wasn't the only issue. I had a short fuse, too.

The tendency to distance myself from others merged with my lack of social and emotional immaturity, resulting in an infantile temper and a propensity to fall into depression over the most inconsequential experiences. In other words, I was a hot-headed crybaby that people didn't enjoy being around. So, the cycle would continue.

Thankfully, God helped me find a way out of this downward spiral. Success in track served as the spark that shattered the self-doubt within me, allowing the slow process of social, emotional, and intellectual maturity to blossom. Like a long rope being extended to someone trapped in a deep, dark pit, winning races—and the acknowledgment that followed—pulled me upward to a place of confidence. I became accepted by my talented teammates, respected by the coaches, and praised by others. And it all started with that first race, one that created a pivotal change in the direction of my life.

However, not everyone gets a chance to win the 400-meter hurdles. But make no mistake, God will always present you with opportunities to change for the better. He will open doors that we can choose to ignore or embrace and *run* through. He will drop a rope for us to grab ... or one that we leave hanging. It is these moments that make the difference—that allow a person to stagnate or move forward onto the path God has created.

Unfortunately, many will fail to acknowledge such opportunities.

Depression

Low self-esteem is like driving through life with your hand-brake on.

—— Maxwell Maltz

The consequences I experienced are not specific to me. Many who carry the burden of low self-esteem will likely experience similar developmental delays, or even permanent damage to social, emotional, and intellectual health. A severe lack of self-worth inhibits progress—it quiets potential. Like a straitjacket restrains a person from movement, so too does low self-esteem suppresses one's ability to optimally experience life. A person can become a prisoner, locked behind bars of self-doubt while ignoring their true worth. A low sense of self-esteem brings with it a downward spiral of destruction that is difficult to reverse. It can inhibit our capacity to learn new things, stunt our ability to adapt to challenging situations, destroy careers, and disrupt relationships.

People with low self-esteem often ignore or downplay their positive qualities and contributions. Like trying to catch water with a strainer, compliments don't stay with a person suffering from depression. They rarely, if ever, feel worthy of praise and fall into describing themselves negatively. They will avoid taking credit for achievements, and instead redirect the praise—not out of humility, but because they simply cannot allow themselves to believe they're worthy of compliments. Those who suffer from depression will also be passive or submissive and overly sensitive to criticism.

Although many people suffer from this debilitating view of themselves, it's not easy to spot those who are hurting. But there are telltale signs in a person who hasn't quite realized how valuable they are.

Reflections

What we feel on the inside is reflected to the world around us. Emotions, perceptions, opinions, and ideas are not entirely invisible. If one believes themselves capable, they will exude confidence. If a person is convinced that they have little value, then that low self-esteem will be conveyed. Feelings are often like a shadow that accompanies us, perceptible to all.

The signals we emit to the world define how the world treats us. If a person radiates low self-esteem, people will often tap into that—perceiving that the person they see has little to no value. If a person behaves in ways that demonstrate confidence, those they encounter will forge a faith that he/she is indeed capable. There's a pleasant truth in this phenomenon; we can *teach* others how to treat us by how we treat ourselves. We have control of how we're perceived by the world and therefore have some control over how we're regarded. And if we don't understand the power we have, we become susceptible to *being* controlled.

Predation

Low self-esteem makes one vulnerable to manipulation. Since our thoughts become evident in our behavior, a person who lacks confidence will appeal to the schemers of the world. Timidity, shyness, and hesitation—if rooted in low self-esteem—will attract marauders. This is a natural phenomenon found throughout nature, where predators target what they believe to be weak prey. It's survival of the fittest; the strong devour the weak. Those that are too frail to put up a fight make for easy targets. Depression, anxiety, and fear are call signs for the enemy. Those not confident in their own worth or ability will be targeted and easily influenced by evil men.

A Missed Destiny

Living with low self-esteem causes a person to miss out on their divine destiny. With confidence in their own value, the happy life they are capable of living is possible. But with no recognition of worth, the foundation for joy is missing—and the victim misses out on what *could be*. They get in their own way. A person with low self-esteem is like a lion looking into the mirror and seeing a helpless kitten—they are blind to their own incredible power.

Biblical Review

Having Courage

Paul (the Apostle), understood the struggles we humans face—including the fight to maintain confidence and self-esteem. He knew we would often feel defeated, weak, and just plain tired. He addressed these tendencies in a variety of ways through his many letters. In his letter to those in the city of Philippi, he encourages them.

I can do all this through Him who gives me strength.

— Philippians 4:13

Paul wasn't being an overly zealous fanatic when he suggested we can do *all* things. He means it. But it's not because we, alone, are so capable. It's because he understands that, when our value, worth, and capability are found "through Him," we do become that powerful. A small chihuahua may be hesitant to stand up to a violent neighborhood cat. But if a muscle-bound pit bull is standing behind that chihuahua, defending his every move, he knows the bullying cat is no longer a threat. In the same way, we who understand the power we have with God can no longer feel intimidated or degraded by the outside world. We can be confident in His power flowing in and through us. Doing "all things" includes being at peace amidst even the most ferocious storms of life. It means we understand our *value* and *competence*, founded in the Almighty.

And make no mistake, He is with us. In the Old Testament, God speaks about how we should have confidence in His presence.

Have I not commanded you? Be strong and
courageous. Do not be afraid; do not be discouraged,
for the Lord your God will be
with you wherever you go.

— Joshua 1:9

Our value is found through, and only through, "Him."
Our confidence and self-worth are tied together,
simultaneously bolstered when we recognize *who* created us.
Without God, we *are* weak. It's of paramount importance that
we understand this. Knowing the love of God and how it
translates into realizing our own worth and capability is the
perfect fuel to keep us confident in not just who we are, but
whose we are.

Though an army besiege me, my heart will not fear;
though war break out against me,
even then I will be confident.

— Psalm 27:3

The Solution

Our Mistakes
If we were asked to list a few past failures, many of us would
not hesitate to find answers. We have no problem digging up
regrets and reliving mistakes. In fact, the challenge may be
keeping our responses to just a *few*. However, if we're asked
to list major victories and accomplishments, we would likely
find ourselves a bit more challenged. It's much easier, more
natural, for us to recollect failures than wins. We are often so
focused on the negativity of our past that we disregard, or

even miss completely, the blessings in our lives. This is one tendency that can lead to and foster low self-esteem. When a person only recognizes their errors, considers only the mistakes made in life, it's difficult to be confident in an inherent ability to thrive.

And that's exactly what the enemy wants.

The Smart Guy

I remember the day it happened. A fellow student, a girl I didn't recognize, approached me in the foyer after class. "You're that smart guy, aren't you?" she asked. I was confused. She must have had the wrong guy. I just stood there, unable to justify her comment. I didn't recall ever being labeled as "smart." But then I remembered the question our professor, Dr. Croy, had offered the class just minutes before. We had been posed, referencing the famous bronze sculpture of a man (Dante) by Auguste Rodin, with: "Where is *The Thinker* looking?"

"He's looking into hell!" I had shouted, to which Dr. Croy nodded in approval.

I only knew that because we had been warned that Dr. Croy might ask questions about the sculpture, and I had taken the time to do a bit of research the night before.

Years earlier, I wouldn't have bothered. For a long time, I was convinced that I was *not* intelligent—and subsequently didn't see much point in putting up a fight about it. I had succumbed to the idea that I was an imbecile, that there was no use in trying to be one of the intelligent kids. However, the confidence I gained from success in track had spilled over into other areas of my life, including academics. The belief in my ability to run fast led to trusting my ability in everything else. I started to *try* to be smart—and it worked. That studious approach would, eventually, lead to a doctoral degree.

There is an interesting irony in this first memory of being considered "smart." *The Thinker,* which served as the inspiration for this book cover, is looking down into the gates of hell—pondering distress and damnation. Many people live with similar perspectives, looking only at their past mistakes, failures, disappointments, or what they believe to be unchangeable traits. They are always looking down, unable to see what's around them. They fail to recognize their place in the world, which is a position of value, acceptance, and significance.

Something needs to change.

It is important that we do not allow lies about ourselves to take hold. Too often we will hear a negative comment, read a negative report, or be put in a situation that makes us feel inferior—and we accept it as truth. So many people live fully convinced that they're unimportant or unworthy in some way; they are wrong. Like some act of evil hypnosis, people often succumb to false ideas about themselves, entranced by thoughts of mediocrity. Sometimes they hold onto those inaccurate presumptions for a lifetime. It takes a paradigm shift, a swing in perspective to break the spellbinding power of despair.

What have you been hypnotized by? Are you convinced you can't get in shape? Are you certain you will never meet that one, special person to spend the rest of your life with? Do you feel you can't break an addiction, be accepted by that school, or get that job? Are you convinced you will always be poor, broken, and defeated? Whatever it is that you have believed is "wrong" with you, put it at the forefront of your mind. It's going to be addressed, so get ready.

Adjust Your Perspective

Sometimes we need to expand our gaze. We need to zoom out and stop hyper-focusing on what the enemy has convinced us is worth worrying about. The mistakes we've made are not nearly as significant as we believe, and concentrating on them will inhibit us from recognizing what can bring us joy. We need to appreciate the lessons of our past, our capability in the present, and our confidence in the future. Satan wants us counting regrets; God wants us to count blessings.

Social media doesn't make this any easier. Inevitably, what we see on Instagram, Facebook, YouTube, and whatever else blurs reality. We find ourselves stung by the tendency to compare our reality to the misrepresentation of someone else's. And before we know it, our lives seem direly inadequate. We find alluring those who constantly praise themselves via these platforms, comparing ourselves to the glorious lives we *think* they have, blinded by their excessive narcissism. Although ancient writers never faced the calamity of TikTok, they knew full well the human propensity to be hindered by comparison—and the foolishness of the models.

We do not dare to classify or compare ourselves with some who commend themselves. When they measure themselves by themselves and compare themselves with themselves, they are not wise.

— 2 Corinthians 10:12

Self-glorification is for fools.

Tips for Redirection

For those deeply entrenched beneath a conviction of worthlessness, the transition won't be easy. It takes time and distance for a train to reverse direction—and maintaining confidence in one's self-worth will take deliberate attention and effort. Self-esteem is not easily transformed. However, it *is* possible. Here are a few tips on how:

1. Start thinking of yourself as a challenger, not the challenged. When self-deprecating, derogatory thoughts enter your mind, consider yourself a fighter, ready and willing to find good in the bad, light in the dark, and self-worth in the pit of hopelessness. You can't be defeated without your own permission. Over time, a new default reaction to negativity will be established. Your immunity to worldly criticism or doubt will become engrained. You will be immovable. A big part of staying aligned, and living out your divine purpose, is to prevent the downward spiral that is catalyzed by low self-esteem.

2. Remember that you're constantly signaling. Keep confidence in the God-given power, authority, courage, and *value* within you so that the message you are sending to the world will align. Emanating this energy is part of letting God be seen in you. God is not weak, and neither are those with Him. This will also make you less attractive to the predators of the world. Even the most vicious hyenas know better than to attack the strongest *lion*.

3. Realize that you're intelligent ... and act on it. You're not a fool, so limit foolish decisions. Get quality sleep, eat well, exercise regularly, and do not, under any circumstances, latch onto destructive vices (drugs, alcohol, tobacco). Harmful habits are in opposition to what elevates self-esteem. If you find yourself focused or drawn to a damaging tendency, remember to look up. Rely on His strength residing in you to defeat cravings for ruin.

4. Don't compare yourself to others, especially *imaginary* people. This is very difficult to do when scouring social media. No one, not a single person, can be fully understood or accurately assessed by reading digital profiles. Yet, we consistently find ourselves jealous, envious, angry, and depressed after comparing ourselves to those on the screen. However, that person, literally, doesn't exist. We're *valuing* ourselves against mythical versions of that person—their social media edition. No one is perfect, and everyone is struggling with something. Monopoly money isn't real currency, and social media profiles aren't real people.

5. Lastly, and most importantly, have faith that God gave you everything you need to accomplish the missions He's set for you. As you move through life, you'll be called to serve in different ways. Meditating on who God is—and who He says you are—will help you navigate those challenges. Low esteem sometimes comes from focusing too much on us, so put the emphasis on Him, no matter the situation. God is good at meeting us wherever we are at. Pray often, listen, and offer sincere trust in Him—it takes the burden off. Believing that God is in control, and that your value is found through Him, diminishes so many of the pressures that we face on a daily basis. Don't let self-doubt near you. Nip it in the bud. When skepticism of your value starts to creep in, put an end to it by seeking Him.

Katrín Confidence

In 2016, Icelandic CrossFit athlete Katrín Davíðsdóttir solidified herself as the "Fittest Woman on Earth" by winning the CrossFit Games for a second time. Her coach, Ben Bergeron, would later write a book called *Chasing Excellence*, in which he outlined the tactics used to help forge such an accomplished competitor. From examining actual events on the competitive stage, to reviewing principles of mental preparedness, the book thoroughly covers many aspects of elite athlete mentorship. One of the many implements supporting Katrín's path to victory was the application of confidence: "Confidence doesn't come from knowing that you can control the outcome of a given event or moment. It comes from knowing that you control your response to a given event. Confidence is about your competitive drive, your focus, positivity, perseverance, and grit, and whether you can maintain those characteristics when it matters most" (Bergeron 2017).

Consider the close ties between our belief in control, confidence, and self-esteem. By realizing how much control we have in any situation, we achieve a degree of confidence by default. After all, confidence is the extent to which we feel *capable*. That trust in our capability then drives the perception of our own *value*, thereby improving self-esteem. In other words, the realization that we have control of any situation, even if it's only control of our attitude, will enhance self-esteem. If we stay aware of our control, we will fend off the torment of low self-esteem.

We may not ever find ourselves on the main floor of a CrossFit Games stadium. But make no mistake, we're in a crazy, chaotic arena—the one called life. And we will constantly find ourselves choosing whether to embrace *or* deny our response to the turmoil that will inevitably find us. When that happens, we can be confident or afraid. It's up to each of us.

Pick Up Your Mat and Walk

There is a story in the Book of John about a crippled man who Jesus heals near a pool called Bethesda. After He has performed the miracle, Jesus gives a peculiar order. He instructs the newly restored man to "Pick up [his] mat and walk." (John 5:8)

In those days, a "mat," which served as a bed, was little more than a small blanket. In this instance, it was most likely dirty, stinky, ragged, and worth little to nothing. Why, then, did Jesus mention it? Why did He go out of His way to instruct the man to pick it up?

Here's why.

Jesus wanted to make it clear to the newly healed man that living in destitute squaller at Bethesda was no longer an option. He was now healed. Taking up his bed was a symbol of leaving behind that former life. He would never again need to lay helpless in anguish. Walking again was a clear, definitive symbol of his new, improved way of living—a new way of thinking—a new purpose.

Those living with crippling depression can experience this same transformation. They, too, can pick up their mat and walk. But it's a decision they must make. Jesus didn't grab the man at the pool by the arm and pull him to his feet. Instead, Jesus gave the man the power to do so. In the same way, God has given us the power to stand up to destructive, demeaning thoughts. We must us that power to get off the ground, take up our bed, and never return.

Self-esteem and confidence in Him are the ultimate source of confidence within ourselves. *God did not give us a spirit of fear* (2 Timothy 1:7). This means that, if you're experiencing fear/anxiety, it's not of God—it is a dark perception that has been planted within you, and it must be ripped out and thrown away. Even the mighty redwood cannot grow if there's no seed to begin with.

Encouragement

Hypnotherapist Dr. Kate Beaven-Marks outlines two reasons why it's important that she wake people up after bringing them under deep hypnosis (Beaven-Marks 2018). One, she says, is for safety. She wants to ensure her clients are perfectly alert when they leave her office and go out into the world. The second is that it offers a definitive end to the hypnosis—it's a formal awakening. You may be in need of a *formal awakening* right now. Whatever it is that you feel inadequate at, consider this the end of your session. Stop believing the lies. Stop feeling damaged. Stop accepting you are insufficient. Stop looking only at your past mistakes, failures, and disappointments.

Wake up! Whoever or whatever convinced you that you cannot beat that one thing—that session is now over.

You are not a mistake. You were not created at random. You have a divine purpose, a responsibility that no one else on earth can fulfill. Like a single, specialized weapon, you are one of one. There is no B team, no backup, and no secondary protocol. God has blessed you with talent beyond measure, and He's expecting a fruitful return on His investment. However, you must *believe* it. You must know who and what you are. If you consider yourself anything less than divinely inspired, you are underestimating the value you carry. You've been endorsed by the same creator of the trillions of unimaginably complex galaxies. To have low self-esteem is to be blind to this truth. *You are God's chosen.*

Let me be clear.

You are:
… smarter than you think.
… better looking than you think.
… more athletic than you think.
… more creative than you think.
… more accomplished than you think.
… more appreciated than you think.
… more artistic than you think
… more respected than you think.
… a better parent than you think.
… a better friend than you think.
… a better son/daughter than you think.
… more *capable* than you think.
… *worth more than you think*.

You have everything you need to live the life of peace that God has outlined for you. Go run your race. And don't worry if the blocks slip, just get up and keep running.

IT'S A PROCESS

CHAPTER 5

HUMILITY

Pride is your greatest enemy,
humility is your greatest friend.

— John R. W. Stott

The Devil's River

During the summer of 2011, my wife and I were at the end of our quickly unraveling rope. We didn't communicate, we weren't happy, and dare I say, we did not love each other. Like a starving, emaciated gazelle lays hopelessly in the desert sand, so too was our commitment—moments away from certain death. Divorce was all but inevitable. Drenched in concern, I wondered how our young daughter and son would deal with the fracture. It was at this time in life that my good friend Jerry, whom you met in Chapter 3, invited me to serve as a groomsman in his upcoming wedding.

It was a long, bumpy ride to the riverside venue tucked deep in the treacherous, rocky canyons of southwest Texas. Prophetically, the ceremony was to be held on the bank of the Devil's River, a striking landscape that, to this day, stands as one of the most stunning I've seen—bright blue water and green flora resting in the foreground of regal grey mountains. The bride's family had just refurbished a beautiful getaway house within walking distance of the river, and everyone was excited to relax and celebrate. My wife was 160 miles away at our home in San Marcos, pregnant with our second child, miserable and alone. Selfishly, I looked forward to escaping the reality of my marital dilemma for a few days.

The first several hours at the river house were spent meeting, greeting, and soaking up the majestic scenery. The father of the bride, Mark, was a short, focused man. His never-smile demeanor combined with a clean, grey flattop conveyed a military nature. It turns out he was not a Veteran, but rather chiseled by a lifelong career in the West Texas Oilfield. Mark's wife, a middle-aged woman who could have easily passed as a Shania Twain doppelgänger, was beautiful and charming—quick to laugh, free with compliments, and making everyone feel welcome. The bridal party was relatively small. Only three bridesmaids, three groomsmen, and a few others had been invited to the picturesque ranch.

Not long after we settled in, the bridal party was looking anything but official. The formal attire I had endured on the journey there transitioned to old flip-flops, faded swim trunks, and a dirty, asymmetrical cowboy hat. Everyone else followed the conversion to casualness—and we headed to the water.

Jessica

It didn't take long for me to notice her. She was aesthetically perfect. Her small, athletic physique was everything a man's primitive lust thirsts for. Long dark hair, captivating eyes, and a beautiful smile complimented her perfect curves; a bright yellow bikini left little to the imagination. She was what shameless fantasies are made of. As the group relaxed on the riverbank, delighting in the cool water at our feet and warm sun on our backs, she made her way over next to me. Her name was Jessica.

"So, you're married?" she softly asked.

"Yep," I said, nodding slowly—as if I wasn't sure.

"That's too bad. Is she here?"

Her body language made it clear that she wasn't curious to meet Lauren, and certainly not concerned with my unborn child within her. Jessica was hunting.

Her boldness was intriguing, mysterious, and sexy. But for a man in my situation, it was also dangerous. I was miserable in my marriage and desperate to feel wanted. Now, sitting next to a gorgeous, willing woman, I felt encompassed by temptation—and Jessica knew it. She thrived on it. My natural tendency to be flirtatious only compounded the problem. My marriage was hanging by a thread, and Jessica was handing me a knife.

Over the next three days (and nights), I did all I could to resist the temptation. But Jessica did not make it easy. Each day she grew bolder, going so far as voicing her desire to be a stepmother to my children. My selfishness was tested, pushed to its absolute limit. I was fighting an insatiable lust, riding an emotional roller coaster, and on the losing side of a spiritual battle. It's a cruel irony how the celebration of Jerry's commitment to his new bride would test the final fragments holding my own fragile matrimonial promises together. However, at the root of it all, Jessica wasn't the problem. I was. The real reason I found myself wrestling with soul-crushing desire was catalyzed by a different fault entirely, a line I had crossed years before.

Me, Myself, and the Tyrant

There's a big difference between confidence and arrogance, but, a thin line separates them. Often one can look like the other. We must know this line—have a keen understanding of what distinguishes self-confidence from conceit, as it will influence the degree to which we succeed in life. That is, the extent to which we follow our divine purpose.

As reviewed in Chapter 4, confidence is the level of trust a person has in his/her own ability. Arrogance, however, is a sense of superiority, an *overestimation* of one's worth or importance. Confidence must be coupled with a sense of humility. Otherwise, that paper-thin line is crossed and all that remains is conceit. Arrogance is a toxic pride, and at Jerry's wedding, my soul was desperately contaminated.

Like many children, my adolescent life was filled with dark, destructive emotions. As I grew, and began to experience achievement in various aspects later in life, trust in my ability improved. The All-American honors, a smokin' hot girlfriend, and the promise of a doctoral degree all boosted my self-confidence. But I went too far, I crossed the line. Just like a race car driver can overcorrect while attempting to avoid a collision—only to suddenly find him/herself in an equally perilous situation—I made an "overcorrection." I let what I considered praiseworthy accomplishments push me too far in the opposite direction, transforming my sense of worthlessness and lack of confidence into something else— something equally dark and destructive. I became an arrogant bully, nothing short of an egotistical tyrant.

My Marriage

The first few years of our marriage are hard for me to discuss, even now. What I reveal here is embarrassing, uncomfortable, and painful. It hurts to admit who I was. But heartache yields lessons engrained, and I can only hope others can learn from my mistakes. My conceit opened the door for the enemy to come in and do his work—and work he did, effectively. Pride caused me to be blind to my duty, ignorant of my purpose, and unwilling to fulfill the promise I made to my bride. Like a ship without a rudder, I veered off course. But it wasn't an abrupt change. Much of what I had become was a slow burn—a patient, calculated sneak attack on my character by the enemy. However, it wasn't the enemy that ultimately transformed me from a timid, cowering adolescent to a self-absorbed aggressor. That was my decision—and there is no person, demon, or God that I can put the blame on. It was all me, I was the one who crossed the wrong line.

In marriage, my actions didn't align with my vows. I was demeaning and disrespectful, malicious and impatient. I refused to accept blame for my mistakes and constantly demanded perfection from my wife. The words I had spoken when I *committed* myself to Lauren were fabricated. My promise "to love and to cherish" was unabashedly conditional on the premise that I remain the priority. That's what pride is.

It's a condition, an ignorant belief that the self is the pinnacle of importance and that others are somehow inferior, even the bride who is supposed to be prioritized. But it's impossible to put someone else at the top when the spot is already taken. There's only room for one.

Humility versus Conceit

Pride: The Seed that Grows

In America, we are subliminally *instructed* to be self-centered. Under various guises, we're taught to believe that we deserve more praise, sympathy, opportunity, resources, respect, and even love than others. However, the propaganda isn't healthy. We are being fed poison. Arrogance is a debilitating toxin that causes our character to decay. If not put in check, that rot will spread.

> *Our society encourages us to put our own needs first.*
> *Many of our current social problems stem from this*
> *glorification of self.*

—— Barbara Killinger

God had been gracious enough to bless me with many gifts that pulled me from the pit of depression. Athleticism, intelligence, wonderful friends, and a beautiful bride were all invaluable treasures *given* to me. But I let them go to my head, allowing my confidence to bleed over into haughtiness. I failed to acknowledge Him as my provider and instead celebrated myself, becoming an egotistical tyrant who demeaned and devalued others. My arrogance infected every aspect of my life, embedding itself into my very personality.

In doing so, I compromised priceless relationships—and I didn't even see it coming.

That's how narcissism works. It starts small, like a boost to the ego that, if not countered with humility, can grow large. If we fail to notice that slight, seemingly insignificant seed of pride, it can blossom into a very destructive mentality. It can embed its roots deep into all that we are and constrict our ability to live out God's good will. And there's a perverse irony about narcissism. The more immense our arrogance becomes, the more likely we will experience disaster. Like the alluring "song of the sirens," as we push closer to the sense of superiority, we are drawn nearer to our doom. Pride is not just unhealthy, it's dangerous. This is what happened to me. Jessica would never have been a threat if I had been humble enough to see the wonderful person my wife was. I had allowed the roots of pride to entangle my heart, making me vulnerable to attacks by the enemy.

A Full Cup

Vain men never hear anything but praise.

—— *The Little Prince*, Antoine de Saint-Exupéry

Just as you can't add water to a glass that is already full, you can't coach someone who thinks they know the game better than anyone else. Arrogance leaves a person at capacity. That's why we say a person is *full* of pride. Ego prevents us from learning. It's a cruel paradox in which the one most in need of help rejects counsel. Pride builds a wall between the victim of self-absorption and a recognition of their own ignorance. The quickest way to fail miserably at life is through blind, uninhibited arrogance.

You cannot get better if you're
convinced you are the best.

— *Ego is the Enemy*, Ryan Holiday

Philautia

The Ancient Greek word *philautia* translates roughly into *a love of self* (this is NOT to be confused with "fellatio"—they are two, *totally* different words). Some consider *philautia* to be healthy, a necessary virtue for mental well-being. In this way of thinking, a vigorous respect for oneself contributes to *confidence*. From another perspective, self-love can be considered inflated ego, and thought reprehensible. It's a "paper-thin line" that distinguishes the two.

We can teeter on this proverbial line. On the one hand, we need to remain confident, and indeed "love" ourselves. Jesus Himself said, *"Love your neighbor as yourself"* (Matthew 22:39). On the other hand, we need to fight our childish tendency to take the love of self too far. It's a struggle to override what Ryan Holiday, called "that petulant child inside every person, the one that chooses getting his or her way over anything or anyone else" (Holiday 2016, 2).

Ultimately, how we define *philautia* doesn't matter. What is important is that we understand that the delicate balance must be recognized and managed. We need to remain equally steadfast in our conviction that we are valuable and capable, while maintaining humility and decorum.

Biblical Review

Shame in Pride

> *According to Christian teachers, the essential vice, the*
> *utmost evil, is Pride. Unchastity, anger, greed,*
> *drunkenness, and all that, are mere fleabites in*
> *comparison: it was through Pride that the devil became*
> *the devil: Pride leads to every other vice: it is the*
> *complete anti-God state of mind.*

—— *Mere Christianity*, C. S. Lewis

Mr. Lewis is correct. Pride, ego, arrogance, conceitedness, vanity, narcissism—whatever you want to call it—it's at the center of what makes immoral humans immoral. Think of your own life and the problems of your past. There is a good chance that, for most of them, pride was involved to some degree.

> *When pride comes, then comes disgrace,*
> *but with humility comes wisdom.*

—— Proverbs 11:2

This proverb best describes my experience with pride. I had experienced great shame, a result of my own doing. When I was finally able to take myself out of universe center, God showed me the star in the center of it all: my wonderful wife, who I was so close to losing. It was then that I realized how foolish I had been. Wisdom is, in part, a conviction that we are not particularly wise. Conversely, narcissism is folly.

Humility Brings the Good Stuff

*Humility is the fear of the Lord; its wages are riches
and honor and life.*

— Proverbs 22:4

No, this doesn't mean a person will spontaneously win the Powerball lottery when they humble themselves and put God first. It does mean that one can experience and appreciate a different kind of wealth—one that elicits a divine reconciliation, a victory in which winning the jackpot doesn't feel necessary. Despite what the world shouts, wealth has nothing to do with money. It starts with humility, a realization that we're not the only ones here.

*Humble yourselves before the Lord, and he will lift
you up.*

— James 4:10

There is a strange, paradoxical irony about arrogance—it's a worship of self, a celebration of the one who is celebrating—yet it comes with no fanfare. There is no honor in honoring oneself. It's like an announcer proudly introducing a prizefighter to the ring, but *he's* the prizefighter … and there is no opponent opposite him or anyone in the audience. In contrast, to be exalted by God is the pinnacle of accomplishment. It is a celebration that could not possibly be more honorable or justified. Yet, we must be humble, content with *not* being celebrated, for this to take place. We must disregard glory for ourselves to be glorified.

*For all those who exalt themselves will be humbled,
and those who humble themselves will be exalted.*

—— Luke 14:11

The Solution

The Line

As mentioned in Chapter 1, we are perpetually lied to by the enemy. He is persuasive, ruthless, and cunning. He can convince us to withhold compassion, be lazy, ignore those who we love, and perceive ourselves as useless. He can also manipulate us into believing that egotism is a justified, healthy mark of empowerment. Satan blurs that paper-thin line between arrogance and confidence—to the point that it can disappear completely. However, that line *does* exist—whether we see it or not. It sets the boundary between the belief that we have been *fearfully and wonderfully made* against the idea that one is *self-made*. One recognizes that God is the source of our strength, while the other cannot see Him at all. To realize our divine purpose, we need to embrace the former. We must see ourselves as being blessed *with* gifts... not *being* a gift.

There is no greater accomplishment in life here on earth that is more rewarding than fulfilling one's divine purpose. That is, accomplishing the many responsibilities that God has outlined—capitalizing on our God-given gifts. Thus, there is nothing more catastrophic to a person than something that deters him/her from living that purpose. Narcissism is one such deterrent. There are tactics we can use to avoid destructive pride that will derail us, but they are not easily applied, and often uncomfortable. Like a ruptured appendix must be removed for the victim to survive, so too with whatever tempts us to ignore God. Surgery is sometimes in order. Our life depends on it.

Pride and Social Media

> *... for they loved human praise more than praise from God.*
>
> —— John 12:43

As reviewed in Chapter 4, social media is a devastatingly effective weapon against our self-worth, confidence, and hope. It provides a treacherous opportunity for one to be distracted, pulled away from divine purpose. It can feed an ego to the point that God becomes little more than a myth in the eyes of the user. Perhaps you've experienced this yourself. Maybe you have been tempted to use Facebook or Instagram to march down the center of your own parade, only to find the "likes," "follows," and "comments" void of value. Or maybe it feeds your ego, creating a false sense of superiority. In either case, if social media is a threat to your humility, cut it out. Like the appendix, it's too small, too insignificant to threaten your *life*. You do not need digital endorsements. You've already been validated by the creator of the universe.

You were not created to be a slave to drugs, alcohol, prescription pills, infidelity, lying, depression, pride, *or manipulative social software*. But here's the catch: it takes wisdom to recognize the hold that it has on you. A slave doesn't always see the chains. Our own ego, molded by the enemy, can inhibit us from taking that step, from distancing ourselves from what we *falsely* believe connects us to other people in a constructive way.

"Self-Made"

Another thing we can do to remain humble is to convey the source of our ability, to admit that our accomplishments aren't entirely our own doing. This doesn't mean we need to redirect compliments or deny involvement just for the sake of modesty. That's a sign of low self-esteem, which we also want to avoid. Rather, when achievement comes, we can acknowledge that we've been *given opportunity.*

I've been involved in the CrossFit community for more than a decade now. In that time, I have seen countless transformations of people who have used the lifestyle to noticeably renovate their health and physique. From the stay-at-home mother who finally shed those extra pounds, to grandfathers who built the strength to move without a walker, to athletes who competed against the best in the world. I've seen it all firsthand. That said, compliments are common in the CrossFit community—which is a good thing. One woman I know, after losing more than fifty pounds of body fat, responded to the many compliments with something like, "Thank you! I've been working with the nutrition coach for months now, and Megan (her coach) has helped me in the gym!" This is such a wonderful view of accomplishment—an acknowledgment of her own effort *and* the contribution of others. It's combining confidence in ability with the efforts of others. This is healthy humility. However, I have witnessed different responses as well.

Some interactions go something like this, "Wow! Your arms are looking good!"

"I know I look good. Everything's poppin'—it was all me!"

Cue error buzzer.

Be grateful for glorification—but be gracious in how you feel about it, and to whom you give credit. None of us are "self-made". A person who is grounded in humility will have a very different response to a compliment than a person enslaved by arrogance. The former will be grateful, the latter will feel their own inflated ego become a bit more bloated.

Stop the Gossip (Mind Your Business)

Another way to demonstrate humility is to avoid being nosy and gossipy. These are tendencies tied to the ego. Attempting to know and spread "dirt" about others is connected to our perceived need to diminish others to make ourselves appear greater. It's a peculiar dance between insecurity in who we are and our vicious pride—an effort to lessen the value of another to elevate our own. But like the irony that comes with egotistical self-praise, a similar irony arises when we slash at the reputation of another: we are the one that bleeds. Slander is evidence that the enemy is winning the war against us. It is hostility and aggression passed *through* us and onto others. Like a powerful electrical pulse that speeds through steel can burn a victim on the other end, so too can we facilitate the transfer of damaging insults. And no, not all gossip is verbal. The moment you talk or "post" negatively about someone else, you are working for Satan himself.

Disregard the mistakes of others if you can't become a part of the solution. For many, this is incredibly difficult, especially if you are close to the person. I know someone who lives a disastrous life in just about every way imaginable. She's addicted to multiple drugs, has abandoned her children, is a habitual liar … the list goes on. Among those who know her, the whispered conversations of condemnation and ridicule are numerous, and from some perspectives, seemingly justified. I used to join in on the verbal bashing sessions myself—but I knew a change was needed. At first, it was difficult to keep my opinions silent, locked away in the dark tower of my own cynicism. But it is better to destroy a negative thought within oneself than unleash it into the world. Shutting down the ego for the sake of humility is a win. We are not designed to scorn or despise. We are intended, by God Himself, to love.

Unfortunately, some will gossip under a mask of righteousness. But spreading the business of others under the guise of a virtuous prayer group or "concern" conversation is no less evil. Slander is slander and evil words are evil words— no matter the context. I've learned that by distancing myself from any form of gossip, I feel much more at peace, aligned with the purpose God has outlined for me.

But how should we respond when we're the *victims* of "mudslinging"?

(No) Retribution

We are often going to be on the receiving end of gossip. In such cases, we *can* be quick to lose our temper and respond with blind fury. However, our reaction should be anything but ferocity—*if* we have a response at all. When we're slandered it's only pride wanting revenge, since it is only our ego that is bruised. However, the smaller the ego, the less damage done. A person who has balanced confidence in their value with humility in their character is immune to offenses like gossip. How can a person be controlled by insults when there's no place for those slights to gain traction? When you learn someone has insulted you, let it move past and beyond you. Ignore it. Avoid the emotional turmoil that comes with being offended by offering it no regard. This is not just a sign of maturity, but also of wisdom, intelligence, and confidence. Peace is worth the loss of retribution. A lion cares nothing about the opinions of sheep.

If someone is talking negatively about you, it's none of your business.

Humility is Clarity

> *Most people do not listen with the intent to*
> *understand; they listen with the intent to reply.*
>
> —— *Stephen R. Covey*

Like peering through a microscope, arrogance places incredible emphasis on one small aspect of our lives—selfish ambition. If all we see is "me," then what's around us isn't perceived. When we are prideful, we don't notice the struggles others—even our loved ones—may be going through. And if we do, only our apathy is offered. When we are plagued with egotism, we ignore the pains and needs of others, refusing to cultivate relationships unless we are certain they will benefit us in some way. Arrogance puts the self at the center, inhibiting us from sincerely expressing empathy, kindness, and love for others—the antithesis of humility. Intentionally noticing and trying to understand other people is a great way to fend off selfish ambition. We should listen to people, respect them.

It takes sincere humility to care about others. It means we must, for a moment, consider their opinions and ideas as being more important than our own. We should always be willing to listen first ... and maybe second, third, and fourth. There is a reason we have one mouth and two ears. We are designed to love first—to genuinely *want* to help. When we intend to understand and appreciate the perspective of another, we are exemplifying unadulterated love. Who knows, we may be inspired to *act* on what we learn (Chapter 2).

Wash Their Feet

In the Book of John, the story is shared of how Jesus Himself washed the feet of the disciples. At the time, they were not sure why Jesus would take such a seemingly humiliating role. After all, they believed Him to be God in human form, the King of all Kings. In a time when people traveled with open-toed sandals through filthy streets littered with trash, urine, and feces, washing a person's feet by hand was a job reserved for the lowliest class. Nonetheless, the man who was revered as the Savior of the world humbled Himself by carefully washing the feet of each of the disciples, including those of Judas, the man Jesus knew would later betray Him. Jesus' actions teach us not only that we should be willing to humble ourselves, but the degree to which we are called to serve others with meekness. If the King above all kings will kneel to wash excrement off the feet of a man who would betray him, we too should live with humility.

Encouragement

Friend, you are profoundly capable and have immeasurable value. You are extraordinary in the sincerest sense of the word. But you cannot discover your purpose if you're convinced that your uniqueness makes you better or any *more exclusive* than others. Leave room in your cup for modesty. By recognizing those around you as equals, you will hold a humility that can be poured out toward others as a bright, enduring light in the world. Stay confident, but don't allow your assuredness to spill over into a celebration of self. Capitalize on opportunities to put others in the spotlight. Doing so will making you a more loving spouse, more caring parent, and more empathetic friend—all of which will make you, ultimately, more fulfilled.

Cashing in on your value can only happen when you're living in genuine humility, understanding that it's not you who defines, quantifies, or even alters your immense worth. You are at your best when you believe, with all that you are, that the Most High is the source of your strength. Your purpose, your divine destiny, the path outlined for you is far too important to miss due to arrogance, pride, or egotism. With humility we can be the person God has called us to be.

CHAPTER 6

LOVE

Where there is love there is life.

— Mahatma Gandhi

The Epiphany

The small group of gathered athletes and spectators was abuzz. Lauren had just completed a "qualifier" workout in her bid to compete at the high-profile fitness competition called "Wodapolooza" and her performance was beyond stellar. She had done so well, in fact, that all those in the gym had enthusiastically swarmed the floor as the clock hit zero. She was a superstar, and the congratulatory smiles of those who witnessed her performance only scratched the surface of their admiration. Lauren was radiant—and I was in awe.

"She's better than you—better than you've ever been," I thought to myself.

Sometimes the voice in our head is gut-wrenchingly honest. And at that moment, it was right. Looking at her, I didn't see the same woman I had shared a home with for the previous decade. She was more than a wife, more than a mother, more than a housekeeper—more than everything I had ignorantly categorized Lauren to be. I realized she was nothing less than a warrior. For me, it was an epiphany of cataclysmic proportions, a clash against the infantile ego I had been clinging to for so long.

And it all started with an apathetic visit to a CrossFit gym.

Odessa CrossFit

I had traveled Eastridge Road hundreds of times—a short stretch of asphalt on the far, eastern edge of Odessa. On one end stood a gray, aged shopping center littered with small shops of a peculiar variety, including nail and tanning salons, an insurance dude, and Odessa CrossFit. I had heard of this "CrossFit" thing a few years earlier but hadn't given it much thought. When it came to fitness, I was a Globo Gym enthusiast with little patience for anything but loud music, heavy weights, hangin' with the bros, and egotism. Little did I know that God would use that small, unfamiliar gym to change my life in a big way. My curiosity about CrossFit was mild, but at that time I simply didn't have anything else to do. As I turned off Loop 338 onto Eastridge, my eyes caught sight of those yellow, block letters and I thought "Why not?"

I pulled into the parking lot out of sheer boredom. By chance, I walked in just a class that was about to begin. The room, no bigger than a four-car garage, was bustling with twenty or so members getting into formation as a well-organized grid, their backs toward me. The coach, a young woman named Tori, walked over with astute authority and informed me that I was not allowed to participate.

Apparently, I had not "gone through a fundamentals class" and was subsequently unprepared for whatever was about to happen. Insulted, I sat disgruntled on the desk stool to watch.

#Lame

Over the next hour, my bruised ego would take a back seat to my wonderment. CrossFit had everything I enjoyed about working out packed into one, chaotically organized collection of heavy weights, loud music, fast action, and camaraderie. There was even a jacked, shirtless dude with the words "There is no greater hunter than the hunter of man" tattooed across his back—a bro, if I ever saw one. When class was over, I had a very different outlook. Coach Tori approached me.

"Well, what do you think?" she asked.

I looked her in the eye and spoke with the same directness she had flung at me moments before: "I don't care what it takes. I don't care how much it costs. I don't care what the hell 'fundamentals' is. I want in."

A New Interest
Over the next several weeks, I became entrenched in every aspect of my new hobby. The look, the lingo, and every aspect of the CrossFit culture quickly embedded itself within me. It was an addiction … and I was a fiend.

Justin Whitaker, the owner of Odessa CrossFit, was kind and welcoming. A former high school baseball coach turned gym owner, he was desperate to make his new venture a success and justify leaving a steady job to try his hand at entrepreneurship. Justin needed to market his "box", as CrossFit gyms are sometimes referred to—and he needed content to do that. After we got to know one another, he approached me with a proposition.

"Your wife's a photographer, right?" Justin asked.

"Yep. She dabbles in it," I said.

"Do you think she would be willing to take a few pictures every now and then? I need some for our website and social media platforms. If so, I'll offer her a free membership!"

I paused. Past discussions between my wife and me regarding anything related to fitness hadn't gone well.

"I really doubt it, man," I told him. "She's never shown interest in working out. But you can ask."

Justin did ask. And, to my surprise, Lauren agreed.

God Works with Stupid

For years, Lauren's apathy for anything "exercise"—combined with my monstrous ego—caused only heartache for both of us. She did not enjoy traditional workout regiments, and especially detested my persistence in bugging her to partake. For years I had not-so-lovingly attempted to coerce her into adopting a life of fitness, with only a damaged marriage to show for it. Even after I had been "CrossFitting" for several months, Lauren had shown no interest in it, and I was certain that wouldn't change. In retrospect, I can't blame her. A wife does not want to hear that she's inadequate—and certainly doesn't want to be forced into anything. How fervently stupid I was.

Thankfully, God can work with anyone, even the fervently stupid.

A Warrior Arises

Lauren would periodically attend CrossFit classes, taking various pictures that Justin would use to market his business. She wasn't necessarily excited about trying CrossFit, but considering it was free, she reluctantly succumbed to her own curiosity. Lauren eventually took a bite … and she enjoyed it. For the first few months, Lauren and I didn't go to the same classes. She would go in the morning, and I would hit the CrossFit workout of the day, or "WOD," each afternoon. Nonetheless, CrossFit became a connector—a glue to which we were both attached. As time went on, something wonderfully strange and unexpected began to happen. Yes, her body began to transform physically, but a more important change was occurring. We started communicating. CrossFit became that conversational piece we could both relate to. A bit of goodness began to bloom again in our frail marriage.

After several months, the changes became more pronounced. Lauren continued to get physically stronger, faster, and fitter. But these external adaptations were only public displays of an inner strength that was building. Lauren's courage, tenacity, and resolve skyrocketed. Her self-esteem, which had been all but eradicated due to my intolerable arrogance, began to emerge. Like a crushed butterfly slowly gaining the strength to fly again, my wife was coming back to life. My blinders began to slip away, too. Like a curtain being slowly pulled back to allow light to stretch across a darkened room, I started to see my wife—really see her. And then came the moment when the dam holding back my denial and pride collapsed. I realized the courage Lauren had always possessed, the grace she offered without hesitation, and her unbreakable spirit. I began to see the immense, paradoxical life I had been living—that the villain in the story of our wrecked marriage was me. I realized she was indeed "better than me," and that it had nothing to do with how physically fit she was. I had been a tool (pun intended) used by the enemy, manipulated and living in desperate conceit.

God had used generic yellow, block letters in a rundown shopping center to counter my calamitous failure—to share a wisdom that had been sorely lacking in my life. He made it abundantly clear that my wife is the most precious, valuable gift I have ever been blessed with. If only I had been wise enough to take myself off the pedestal, then I could have offered the respect and affection that my wife deserved. At the root of the distance and tension was my failure—my lack of love, the *real love* that is needed to make a relationship work.

Again, God works with stupid.

Where's the Love?

What Goes into the Cup

> *... God is love.*
>
> —— 1 John 4:8

As mentioned in Chapter 5, we are containers. We can pour out into the world only that which has first filled us. I was unable to demonstrate love for my wife because I had not first put love within me. And since God is love, my inability to show patience, kindness, and forgiveness was rooted in the absence of *God* within me. I had filled my cup with selfishness; there was no room for Him.

Without God (love), we cannot live out our God-given purpose. We can't let our light shine if there is no light inside of us. Unfortunately, I'm not the only one who has failed to fill the cup appropriately.

The lack of love is everywhere.

(Love) Misguided

My mother's second husband, David, worked as a carpenter outside of Greenville, a small town northeast of Dallas. They married when I was about seven, and up to that point in my life, my mother had shown a bold acceptance for all people: Jew, Gentile, black, white, democrat, republican—she didn't care. She respected everyone. However, David did not see things the same way. From the moment I met him, he was constantly revealing his contempt for African Americans, often using the "n" word to express his animosity. So, being the young boy who wanted to impress his *new* dad, on the first day of school I picked a fight with the first black kid I saw. We both got sent to the principal's office.

Thankfully, David was out of my life soon enough and I would avoid being indoctrinated in intolerance. However, many children are raised in similar (or worse) conditions, where they are encouraged to embrace bitterness, envy, or jealousy. From a young age, some families are conditioned to make negative assumptions based on skin color, sexual orientation, religious beliefs, age, gender, and whatever else— and their cups begin to fill. Parents or other respected elders teach children the lies they have adopted, and that same mentality is passed on—all under the guise of loving guidance. This is a very dangerous cycle, where the same darkness is poured from cup to cup, generation to generation. It's important that we consider deeply *how* we love and what we are basing our instructions on. It is vital that we consider what we are pouring into others.

Bigotry is *not* Christ-like love.

Agape

The ancient Greeks had multiple words for what we have isolated into one "love." This allowed them to clearly distinguish which type of interest or affection was being directed from one person to another entity. That way, there was no confusion between the passion for a favorite vegetable soup and the emotion a father had for his son. Well done, Greeks.

Eros, ludus, philia, storge, philautia, pragma, and *agape* are each a distinct form of love that has certain emotions tied to each. *Agape* (Greek, ἀγάπην)—now acculturated into English—is sprinkled throughout the various denominations of the Christian faith. In essence, *agape* references the greatest degree or form of *true* love of another. It's not an admiration of self (*philautia*), nor a description of a friendly bond (*philia*), but an absolute, sacrificial passion that persists regardless of condition or circumstance.

It's this *agape* that we're missing in the world—the "love" that has been butchered and misused over time.

Saying "Love"

> *Love is the most important word in the English language—and the most confusing.*
>
> — Gary Chapman

How many times have you said that you *love* a specific food? How often do we hear someone reveal *love* for an activity such as hiking, a pet, or a place? In modern culture, the word "love" is used to describe just about any degree of fascination, from the immense commitment a mother has for her child to one's beer preference. We have bastardized the word, blurring its sanctity. No matter how broad or specific one chooses to define it, there's one thing that's certain: We "love" a lot, but we don't *love* nearly enough.

Every time my wife and I speak on the phone, we end the conversation with "Love you, bye." We say it casually, without thought; it is a habitual response expressed without enthusiasm. Sometimes my wife or I will tell one of our children "I love you" in a similarly lukewarm tone, almost a knee-jerk reaction to a parting of ways. However, no matter how monotonous or repetitive we use the word "love" with one another, we do not minimize the purity of what it means. We've trained ourselves to refrain from claiming the same feeling for anything that we don't sincerely love, like a type of food, place, pet, or whatever else. This lets our children know that we take the word, and its meaning, seriously. They know that they are not categorized with any insignificant place, thing, or idea. When Lauren or I say "love," we mean it.

I encourage you to adopt a similar practice. Don't use "love" if you don't want to convey a deep, meaningful affection. This is a way to get one of the most under/overused words back on track, to put sanctity back into "love."

Biblical Review

Love is Patient …
If you've been to Christian weddings, you are probably familiar with the passage in Paul's letter to the church in Corinth that defines love:

Love is patient, love is kind. It does not envy, it does not boast, it is not proud. It does not dishonor others, it is not self-seeking, it is not easily angered, it keeps no record of wrongs. Love does not delight in evil but rejoices with the truth. It always protects, always trusts, always hopes, always perseveres.

— 1 Corinthians 13:4-8

Can you guess which Greek word is used in the ancient translation of this verse? Answer: ἀγάπην (*agape*) Interestingly, this same word is used to describe God's love for us! This means that the unbridled, unconditional commitment that God has for each of us is the exact same dedication we should show to others. This is how *God is love.* He pours Himself into us, and we then become equipped to express that same immense patience, trust, hope, and kindness.

God-sourced *agape* is what we need to constantly be pouring in, so that we can pour Him out.

The "Law"

If I have the gift of prophecy and can fathom all mysteries and all knowledge, and if I have a faith that can move mountains, but do not have love, I am nothing. If I give all I possess to the poor and give over my body to hardship that I may boast, but do not have love, I gain nothing.

— 1 Corinthians 13:2-3

If we cannot love each other, our efforts in life are woefully wasted. It doesn't matter how big the house, how deep the pocketbook, how long the friends list, or how well-known our name—if we are missing love, we are derailed and distanced from our divine purpose. I can *claim* to care about people. I can even write a book about the importance of honesty, compassion, work ethic, and humility—all wrapped neatly with a ribbon of Christ-like doctrine. But if I do not love people, it's all just distractive noise.

So, who exactly are we instructed and called upon to apply this patience, kindness, and truth toward? Who are we to "never fail?!" Who all should we *love*? Jesus tells us.

> *Hearing that Jesus had silenced the Sadducees, the Pharisees got together. One of them, an expert in the law, tested him with this question: 'Teacher, which is the greatest commandment in the Law?' Jesus replied: 'Love the Lord your God with all your heart and with all your soul and with all your mind.' This is the first and greatest commandment. And the second is like it: 'Love your neighbor as yourself.' All the Law and the Prophets hang on these two commandments.*

— Matthew 22:34-40

Being asked to identify the "greatest commandment" is, in my opinion, a justified question. And it's with a great sense of urgency that we should consider, and act on, His answer. Jesus said "all" the law hangs on *loving God and loving others*. This means that, if we don't follow these two rules, we are breaking the very foundation of who we are called to be and how we are called to live. Loving God is to love others, and loving others is to love God. There is not one without the other.

No matter what we do in life, if we fail to love, we are failures.

But love, *agape* love, is difficult.

It's Hard ...

> *Father, forgive them, for they do not know what they are doing.*
>
> — Luke 23:34

Loving can be tough. Can you really remain patient with *all* your family and friends? Can you be *slow to anger* with people that you resent? Can you "keep no record of wrongs" with that one person who is a blaring prick? What about those who have cheated or lied to you?

If He can, we should too.

One of the most profound displays of love comes from the Gospel of Luke. While hanging on a Roman cross, suffering unimaginable torture, Jesus prayed for the men executing Him—those who were deliberately killing Him in the most cruel, demeaning way possible. With what little breath Jesus could muster, He asked God to forgive the soldiers. As in, to completely overlook atrocity.

Thankfully, we will not be called to demonstrate incredible love and forgiveness while hanging from a Roman cross. But make no mistake, our divine path *does* include loving others no matter how different their beliefs may be from ours or how they treat us. We must be so confident in our commitment to God, to our purpose, that we can consider *all* people as worthy of God's love, and therefore worthy of ours as well.

The Solution

Love in Marriage

> *For this reason a man will leave his father and mother*
> *and be united to his wife,*
> *and the two will become one flesh*

— Jesus (Matthew 19:5)

Marriage can be tough—especially if you're married to someone like me! One reason marriage is so difficult is because we are hard-wired for selfishness; it is literally a survival instinct. However, a healthy marriage requires a program override. Each spouse should consider the others' happiness, comfort, and security as being just as vital, and sometimes more so, than their own. Each must fully respect the others' opinions, ideas, perceptions, preferences, and boundaries. In every part of the social engagement—from eating habits to sex to stress management to hobbies—there's a delicate dance that occurs when both husband and wife *genuinely* commit to one another. As time goes on, and this "dance" is navigated, the two may find themselves fully encompassed and dependent on the other, part of a relationship forged in trust and reliance. It's this connection that Paul references when he writes that the couple will "become one flesh."

However, many have criticized or even rejected the biblical view of marriage altogether. One passage in particular has resulted in an incredibly inaccurate interpretation of the scripture. Let's consider this section from Paul's letter to the people of Ephesus.

> *Wives, submit yourselves to your own husbands as you do to the Lord. For the husband is the head of the wife as Christ is the head of the church, his body, of which he is the Savior. Now as the church submits to Christ, so also wives should submit to their husbands in everything.*

—— Ephesians 5:22–24

This instruction by Paul about the responsibility of a wife can ruffle feathers. My own wife, Lauren, is strong, determined, and fiercely independent. The moment I expect her to unquestionably "submit" to everything I say is the moment I'll be sleeping on the couch—or worse. However, like many scriptures of the Christian Bible, this portion is taken far out of context. The problem is that many do not try to appreciate what Paul is teaching. These verses are not fully understood, in large part, because many who extract "wives, submit to your husbands" fail to continue reading and fully grasp the picture being painted by the author. Let's read on.

Husbands, love your wives, just as Christ loved the church and gave himself up for her to make her holy, cleansing her by the washing with water through the word, and to present her to himself as a radiant church, without stain or wrinkle or any other blemish, but holy and blameless. In this same way, husbands ought to love their wives as their own bodies.

— Ephesians 5:25–28

The husband is called to accept an incredibly daunting role regarding the "submission" outlined for the bride. Just as Jesus became a servant to the church (people), and literally gave His life for it, a husband must fully and unconditionally love his bride. He must place her well-being above his own. This is an incredibly powerful and meaningful synergy that is rooted deep in the gospel itself, where a wife allows a man to take responsibility for her, and the husband uses that responsibility to abandon his own selfish agenda. There is an immense obligation of *both* parties to prioritize the other. A marriage commitment that is biblically based occurs when each spouse is wholeheartedly devoted to the other. It's this Christ-like assurance that protects against the inevitable challenges that a couple will face after the honeymoon phase. If both husband and wife fully embrace the immense responsibility outlined in the Book of Ephesians, a divine fortress will envelop the marriage, making their love impervious to the many predictable attacks of the enemy. When the initial rush of romance is gone, it is important that it be replaced by *agape* (unconditional) love.

Friends and Family

Years ago, I sat on the couch watching the movie *Ocean's Eleven*, holding my sleeping infant daughter McKinlee. As the film came to a close, she began to rustle from sleep. I stood and began to rock her gently while the credits rolled down the screen and music played. I studied her small, beautiful face. I'm not sure what it was, because I already knew that I adored her, but at that moment I was overcome with a fierce, overwhelming sense of affection—*real*, unrestrained love. Like some of you may have experienced, I felt an emotion so powerful it cannot possibly be articulated. Would I protect her, fight for her, nurture, teach, and provide for her? Absolutely. Would I die for this little girl? A thousand times, yes. In that quiet, peaceful moment, I felt like God was speaking to me, outlining my clear, defined purpose—to demonstrate an unconditional *love* for this young girl. I was all-in on that assignment.

However, sometimes it's not easy to love our family. Our relatives aren't all infants that we can rock to sleep in our living room or calm with a pacifier. Loving our own family can be a challenge.

A good friend of mine, I'll call him Brad, is the youngest of four boys. His oldest brother has embraced destructive habits that bring chaos, dissension, and malevolence wherever he goes—including family gatherings. On countless occasions, Brad has attempted to provide counsel and encouragement to his brother in hopes of dousing the darkness that his brother brings with him. However, those efforts have failed, and Brad has been forced to decide whether or not to maintain the relationship. Many of us will have to make a similar decision. We will need to choose whether to place ourselves, and possibly our children, in the enemy's shadow by staying involved in the life of someone whom we deeply love. We will need to decide what is more important: fulfilling a tradition of politeness or removing ourselves from a toxic relative's presence. I suggest the latter. Your divine destiny is too valuable, too exclusive a force, to compromise for the sake of tradition. As I once heard a pastor say, sometimes we must love family members from a distance.

Let It Go

If irony ever made its presence known during the Civil Rights Movement of the mid-twentieth century, it was on April 4, 1968, in Memphis, Tennessee. The evening before, the great Dr. Martin Luther King Jr. had delivered what would become known as the "Mountaintop" speech. With it, Dr. King inspired an already passionate crowd to keep fighting against the evil of racism. Part of his eloquent presentation included a reference to the Jericho Road, a dangerous, windy path connecting Jerusalem to Jericho that Jesus Himself used as the setting for the powerful parable mentioned earlier (The Good Samaritan).

The following day, Dr. King was murdered for his role in leading a moral crusade, a victim walking the proverbial *Jericho Road*. But Dr. King left an undeniable mark on his community, his nation, and the world—especially regarding the realm of love.

Returning hate for hate multiplies hate, adding deeper
darkness to a night already devoid of stars. Darkness
cannot drive out darkness, only light can do that.
Hate cannot drive out hate, only love can do that.

— Dr. Martin Luther King, Jr.

Dr. King makes a point that is equally true and difficult to apply. When we are wronged, it's not easy to let it go. Our tendency to reciprocate the offense is a natural reaction. However, an automated response of rage only adds more problems—just as with the reaction to Dr. King's assassination, in which rioting, burning, looting, and vandalism broke out in more than a hundred cities around the country. If we can learn to sincerely be "slow to anger" (Proverbs 15:18), and have love set as our default response, we will find ourselves unshakable. We will be steadfast in peace.

Love can only be held by first letting go of hate.

Keep the Fire Burning

Much like everything in life, the ability, tendency, and desire to love can fade. It is hard to perpetually push against our instinct to care only about ourselves. Just like many who make New Year resolutions and rarely see them through, the desire and motivation to be honest, selfless, patient, understanding, and forgiving can crumble even after we've been inspired in some way. Like a car must constantly have fuel to operate, so too must we continually fill ourselves with love—we've got to keep pouring it in. It's important that we keep that fire burning despite our selfish nature.

For me, I've found that listening to encouraging podcasts, engaging in conversation with kind people, and prayer are great ways to combat envy, disdain, anger, and other destructive emotions. However, when I distance myself from the good in the world, I find myself giving *less good* in return. You can't pour acid into a cup and expect to pour out life-giving water. We should be consistently aware of what we're allowing into our hearts and minds.

Keep the good coming—and going.

Encouragement

According to the Gospel of John, one of the last things Jesus was able to speak before He died on the Roman cross was: "It is finished." (John 19:30) The word recorded in a 4th-century Christian manuscript of a Greek Bible (Codex Sinaiticus) for "It is finished" is the Greek τετέλεσται (*tetelestai*). Interestingly, that same word has been found on ancient bits of papyri from that region and time period to represent a fascinating connotation. It was found that τετέ^λ (an abbreviation for τετέλεσται) was used to denote that a debt had been paid in full (Grenfell 2018). This means that, whatever Jesus actually said, the meaning of "it is finished" holds a much deeper implication than meets the eye. Likely, He said something that would be much more in line with his message of servitude, far more meaningful to a life (and death) of purpose. Jesus, with His last few breaths, let us all know that *our immense debt is now paid.*

It's hard for me to find an example more fitting to describe what love is—*agape* revealed. *Jesus died for you.* Despite our failures, despite our inability to always love God and others, Jesus willingly sacrificed Himself for each of us. He paid our debt. He poured all that He is into us, and now it's our turn to pour Him out.

> *We love because he first loved us.*
>
> —— 1 John 4:19

Love, always.

IT'S A PROCESS

CHAPTER 7

PATIENCE

Patience is the companion of wisdom.

— Saint Augustine

Upton County Night

It's around 2:30 a.m. on a January morning in a dark, desolate desert landscape somewhere south of Midland. It's cold—bitter West Texas cold—and every second of enduring the stinging ice from the night sky seems like a lifetime. I'm wearing heavy, flame-resistant coveralls, cotton work gloves, and steel-toed boots, but the "oilfield tuxedo" does little to counter the freezing temperatures. Jorge, my large Hispanic colleague, is not happy that his *gusano*—that would be me—is slowing the progress of our three-person team. I'm trying to help, but my ignorance is too profound to ignore. This is my first real-life oilfield operation and I'm desperately out of my element. I bend down near a large metal structure called a "blowout preventer" to grab a pipe wrench.

"Bang!"

I clumsily slam my head on the steel edge with such force that I'm instantly disoriented. The pain is a quick, thorough reminder that I wasn't wearing my hard hat. As the dizziness slowly dwindles, an even greater sting begins to set in. Though I have been vehemently suppressing it, I'm being tormented by the decisions that led to this moment. This was a mistake, I don't belong here. I begin to cry.

Professor to Peon

Only a few weeks before this frigid night in the forsaken desert, I had been "Dr. Dean," working as an assistant professor of kinesiology at Texas Lutheran University in Seguin (just east of San Antonio). I wore dress pants, had a nice office, and spent my weekdays giving lectures to intelligent, motivated students. The job wasn't a job at all—it was fun, the kind of career that society tells kids to pursue. For me, it was a rewarding hobby that I just happened to get paid for. Bad days at the office, or classroom, were rare.

My colleagues, Dr. Casi Helbig (an associate professor) and Dr. James Newberry (the department head) exhibited unbridled support. They were more than just coworkers, they were reliable and valued confidants. Just about every part of my life in academics was nirvana. But it was a different story outside the university's walls. I was battling the irrepressible arrogance I mentioned in chapter five—and it wasn't just egotism I was dealing with. I had another, equally destructive vice that would reveal itself in vile form—my obsessive impatience, a fault that was easy to exploit.

You already know about Jessica, the yellow bikini temptress whom I allowed to nearly break the back of my already hobbling marriage. Ironically, at that same wedding, the father of the bride (Mark) offered me a job that, due to my impatience, I couldn't turn down. He had waved a carrot of oilfield money in my face and, because I was in such a hurry to *succeed* in life, I bit down hard. I wanted money, prestige, and all the toys young men dream of—and I wanted them immediately, not willing to trust in God's timing. This was what brought me from professor to peon.

The Fall Continues

The frozen night with Jorge was the beginning of the end for me at my first oilfield job. On April 22, my 33rd birthday, I was called to the office and fired on the grounds that I had a bad attitude—and they weren't wrong. I had let my ego synergize with the echoing regret within me, the result being a vicious hate. I hated that I had left academia, hated that I didn't have more to show for it, and hated that I was failing as a husband/father. When they fired me, it only added to the darkness. I blamed Mark, I blamed the manager who fired me, I blamed everyone—but myself.

Little did I know, this was just the first of many drastic failures.

Over the next several years, I would bounce around through various *careers*—rebounding like a pinball in the machine of the oil and gas industry, unable to find stability. I worked as a truck salesman, commercial real estate director, operations manager, business development specialist, crude oil marketer, and several others—all pursuits from which I was eventually fired or quit after becoming disgruntled. The only thing that didn't change was my impatience. My resistance to trust in God's timing was the common denominator, the one variable that dogged me like a bad virus.

Living with (or without) Patience

Kicking and Screaming
Patience yields progress. Impatience does not.

I've read patience defined as *the degree to which one can accept or tolerate delay without becoming annoyed or anxious and without responding in disrespect or anger*. It's a skill that one can choose to develop—or choose to ignore. This is where I failed catastrophically.

Much of my life can be summarized as the antithesis of patience. I have not passively *accepted delay*. I have not allowed interruption without becoming irrational, destructive, and disrespectful. I have been the *adult* perpetually kicking and screaming when things didn't go my way. But why?

After I experienced a boost in self-esteem from my "success" early in life, there came a self-imposed expectation that wins should come often, easily, and robustly. When that didn't happen—when I was just an ignorant *gusano* banging my head on a hunk of oilfield metal—I began to feel like a failure, something I hadn't been used to being for years. I needed to win, fast. It's funny how an effort to speed things up makes the situation exponentially worse. Sometimes we trip so many times trying to get to the front that we are perpetually behind.

Impatience to Imposter

My effort to speed up the process was rooted in a lack of faith (elaborated on in Chapter 10). I didn't have confidence in God leading me, so I chose to lead myself. I remember playing out this hypocrisy in my mind. I would tell myself (and others) that I was a "believer," a Christian who *follows* the teachings of Jesus Christ. But the only thing I was following was my own, flawed reasoning. I was ignoring God, His word, and His council.

C. S. Lewis once wrote, "There are only two kinds of people in the end: those who say to God, 'Thy will be done,' and those to whom God says, in the end, 'Thy will be done.'" (Lewis, The Great Divorce 1945)

What he means is, God is willing to guide, protect, and lead us if we are willing to heed His word. He loves us enough to let us choose whether or not to trust Him. He will provide us the freedom to follow in faith—or ignore Him and live life on our own terms—making it *our will be done.*

I chose the latter, which is why the pattern of dissatisfaction continued, and why I kept getting cyclically poor results. It doesn't make sense to plant the same seed over and over again and expect a different fruit. But that's exactly what I did. Each time I was derailed by my own impatience I would respond by becoming more impatient.

My perpetual feelings of dissatisfaction led to resentment for the state I was in, which would then be directed toward those around me (often those in a position of authority). I was constantly frustrated, not only convinced I deserved more, but that I should get it faster—and I blamed the boss when that didn't happen. I would become convinced that I was better suited and more capable than others—then when I failed I would resent them. My impatience, fueled by arrogance, is the reason I couldn't settle in. It was the reason I chose to lean on my understanding of what success was— what it took to advance in life.

What a buffoon I was. But I'm not the only one.

Impatience Is Immature

Many people battle impatience. They trudge tirelessly through the swamp of discontentment, frustration, and unhappiness. An *intolerance of delay* often leaves people drowning in regret. Like me, it leads to rash, illogical decisions—responses that are often followed by remorse and shame. The effects of such actions (or *reactions*) can be acute stings resonating over the long term.

So where does impatience stem from?

Have you ever refrained from giving a baby something he/she wants? They don't respond well. Crying, throwing, kicking, screaming, smashing, and yelling are a few responses you can expect when forcing an infant to wait on a toy, piece of candy, or whatever else they've deemed worthy. Impatience is a natural response that humans intrinsically exhibit. But how soon do we mature past the point of kicking and screaming? At what age are we tolerant of delays? Sadly, the degree to which we apply patience doesn't necessarily correlate with time. Impatience is something that can plague a person for a lifetime. It's an infantile tendency that, regrettably, stays firmly rooted in a person's psyche if they don't acquire a proficiency for tolerance. An adult who is constantly at risk of losing their cool from unexpected delays or mishaps is a toddler with an invisible pacifier hanging around their neck. Impatience is immaturity, tolerance is wisdom. But how does one develop patience? How can a person remove the "pacifier"?

Patience Must be Practiced

As mentioned, patience is a *skill*. It can be better understood, practiced, and learned—to the point that it becomes a default setting, overriding the primitive, childish nature within us. However, valiant effort is constantly needed. If we can't learn to *adapt to the overload* of constant and unexpected impediments, we're stuck in a cycle of being overcome by what we perceive as adversity.

When my wife first started CrossFit, she wanted to do more than just be healthy and "in shape." She wanted to compete. Each day, Lauren would try her best, but she wasn't all that good relative to the other women in the class. She had little skill and would often find herself with a low score on the whiteboard, the large panel where each member's results were recorded. But Lauren was committed. She would wake up at 3:50 a.m. to get ready, then make the long trip to the far side of Odessa to get to the early morning class. Day after day she diligently worked on her strength, endurance, and mobility. It was uncomfortable, but she gradually improved and eventually became one of the most decorated CrossFit athletes in West Texas and, eventually, was able to compete with the best in the world. Her patience paid off.

Practice takes patience, and patience takes practice. If we want to mature—to be better—we must make an attentive effort to control our emotions when unexpected delays come before us. But unlike CrossFit, where the testing is voluntary, life will throw delays of all kinds at us, whether we are ready for them or not. Lauren chose to get up early in the morning day after day to test her mettle in CrossFit. Life is going to test our ability (or inability) to remain patient regardless.

A Change is Needed

Practicing patience is not something we're naturally drawn to. To push against that inner child who wants to kick and scream every time something doesn't go their way is difficult. It takes both a recognition of and a confrontational response to our immature way of thinking.

Your life does not get better by chance,
it gets better by change.

— Jim Rohn

Becoming angrily annoyed at delays, whether actual or simply perceived, is catastrophic to one's ability to live happily, purposefully, and content. Each person must take responsibility for themselves. They must be their own catalyst for change, and embrace the wisdom needed to break the destructive cycles that result from a lack of patience. Just as admitting to having a problem is the first step in battling addiction, it takes a level of self-awareness and maturity to recognize that a lack of patience may be wreaking havoc on one's own life. A default reaction to improperly identify outside influences as the source of one's failure will inhibit the truth that the *self* is the real culprit (more in Chapter 9). In other words, sometimes we need to recognize when *we* are the problem.

Wall Puncher

While attending Angelo State University, I had a friend who would constantly get so engulfed in anger he would punch holes in the walls of his apartment. Most of the time, in his childish but violent charades, he would simply thrust his fist through the thin, fragile sheetrock—leaving a large, clean hole in the wall. However, sometimes his knuckles would inadvertently find one of the wall's studs. More than once my short-tempered friend found himself not only on the wrong end of another repair bill, but also sporting a broken hand. I wonder how much pain, medical debt, and sheetrock repair could have been avoided if my wall-boxing friend could have controlled his temper—that is, if he could have been more patient.

But walls (and hands) aren't the only things destroyed by a lack of patience.

Relationships

Not having patience is synonymous with a consistent sense of anxiety. It's a perpetual discontentment, constantly being on edge—an ongoing sense of dissatisfaction. And as such, it is not conducive to social development. When people who have mastered patience find themselves around someone who hasn't, they recognize the disparity. The patient person finds themselves in a situation that is uncomfortable and unpleasant; they will want to distance themselves in order to regain their peace. Just like most adults recognize the immaturity of a child crying over spilled milk, the even-tempered person will notice the ill-tempered. People don't enjoy being around crybabies.

Even the most composed person may be lured to irritation when around a person who is constantly impatient. People can become annoyed by the annoyed and angered by the angry. A person who becomes belligerent at the onset of every delay will potentially pass on that pugnacious response. Those who have little patience are diseased, and they spread their infection to others. This, of course, inhibits so much of what makes quality relationships last. It's difficult to serve as a source of positive inspiration, not to mention being a joy to be around, if every interruption awakens a childish response. And so, a person who is constantly anxious will often find themselves alienated, which only contributes to their anxiety. It's a vicious cycle of the sick getting sicker.

How many relationships have been destroyed by something as trivial as a lack of patience? How many estranged mothers, fathers, daughters, sons, cousins, and friends have been permanently alienated due to an otherwise peaceful person getting fed up?

Impatience breeds anxiety—while patience fosters peace.

Impatience Is Fear

Sometimes impatience masks fear. When a plan is hindered—when what we want seems to be at risk—we become afraid that it may not happen at all. When whatever we are hoping to accomplish is delayed in some way, the ensuing anxiety and frustration are simply a result of fear. We become whole-heartedly convinced that we cannot be content until whatever we want happens—and it needs to happen on our schedule. When doubt arises, the fear of failure sinks its teeth into us. This is what happened to me. When things weren't moving fast enough, I became stiflingly terrified of failure. I wasn't making enough money, I wasn't garnering enough respect, and I didn't have the nice house, the fancy car, or the elite societal status. None of what I wanted was happening in the time frame I had defined. Inevitably, that concern turned to worry which turned to terror. The *want* had transitioned to a perceived *need*. This happens to us all. We live in fear that we will be stuck in a pit of discontentment until we reach that goal, whatever it may be. We have talked ourselves *into* being afraid. I'm hardly a proponent of using Hollywood as a source of inspiration or truth, but perhaps George Lucas got it right when he wrote these lines for one of his most iconic characters:

Fear leads to anger, anger leads to hate,
hate leads to suffering.

— Yoda

Biblical Review

Paul's Points

As mentioned in earlier chapters, the Book of Proverbs is a phenomenal source of wisdom. I encourage anyone, Christian or not, to dig into the treasures hidden within this great work. One particular passage highlights how patience is a sign of maturity.

Whoever is patient has great understanding,
but one who is quick-tempered displays folly.

—— Proverbs 14:29

I believe "folly" is just a humble translation of *stupidity*, which has been my own *proverbial* call sign in far too many instances. A buffoon can pretend to be a wise man for only so long before his/her behavior proves otherwise. Like the stripes on a tiger, eventually a fool's childish nature of impatience will be exposed.

Paul addresses both *hope* and *patience* many times throughout his letters, including his message to the church (people) in Rome. Specifically, he encourages us to expect that which we cannot see—and to calmly wait for it.

But if we hope for what we do not yet have,
we wait for it patiently.

—— Romans 8:25

Too often we fall into the trap of waiting *im*patiently. We hope to get well, be financially free, acquire the nice house, a baby, a spouse, a better career—but we feel anxious, angry, or bitter when it doesn't happen in the time frame we've chosen. That is not waiting "patiently." The wise remain at peace even when they don't notice progress.

Paul continued to teach about patience in that same letter.

Be joyful in hope, patient in affliction,
faithful in prayer.

—— Romans 12:12

This means we're called to be patient, not only when we don't see progress, but even when we seem to be regressing—when the hard times *really* hit. Paul isn't referencing the inconsequential nuisances of life, like a middle-finger maniac at a stop light. He's talking about genuine tribulation (like being hunted, imprisoned, and possibly killed by Roman soldiers, which he had witnessed firsthand). Even in the direst of situations, we are encouraged to hope, to be *patient*, and to pray. When we face incredibly difficult circumstances, that's when patience counts. If Paul, with all his experiences, can advise potential victims of martyrdom to be patient, how much more should we embrace the virtue?

But too many times we try to take matters into our own hands. We ignore God, confident that we alone are strong enough to forge our own path, that *we make our fate* or are *self-made*. I assure you, friends, such a mindset is a one-way ticket to Disappointment Land—and it sucks there. I know because I lived there for years. Invest in patience, and let God put in the sweat equity. Let Him do the heavy lifting.

The Lord will fight for you; you need only to be still.

—— Exodus 14:14

The Solution

Get a Grip

A habit of impatience is the foundation of so many other crippling characteristics. If you cannot wait a few more minutes than you're accustomed to at a restaurant, you'll be tempted to be rude to the waiter. If you're forced to wait at a green light because the person in front of you is staring at their phone, you may want to give them the ol' one-finger "highway hello." Every day, on multiple occasions, we will have opportunities *to become annoyed or anxious*, and to then, subsequently, *respond with disrespect or anger*.

Refrain.

After almost eighteen years of marriage, my wife has called me out more than a few times for behaving hastily. She uses a cliché that perfectly captures respectful rebuke, witty wisdom, and charming chastising.

"Get a grip!" she'll say.

In honor of her eloquent advice, I'll pass that same to you. *Get a grip!* Recognize how *un*important so much of what we worry about is. When Dietrich Bonhoeffer was first thrown in Nazi prison, he noticed a curious comment carved into the cell wall: "In hundert jahren ist alles vorbei" [In a hundred years it'll all be over] (Metaxas 2010)

Put your concerns in the proper perspective. Consider what's worth your worry, anxiety, and frustration. Is what we lose our cool over really worth losing our cool over? The

TikTok addict, the middle-finger bandit, and all the other nuisance nuggets that buzz into our lives are likely more trivial than we treat them. If we really believe that God is in control, we shouldn't be bothered by delay. If we are certain that He is directing our steps, then we should be confident that He can work around any impediments that we were not expecting.

Do You Trust?

Although the concept of trust will be expounded upon in Chapter 10, it's closely tied to our ability to embrace patience. Patience is a measuring stick. It's a barometer for testing the degree to which trust endures. It is a certainty in God's ability, reliability, and strength to beat whatever our problem is. Do you believe that a situation will "be ok" when it's delayed or doesn't happen the way you want it to? Do you really trust that God is in control? If so, you don't need to worry or be anxious about the future. You can be confidently patient no matter the circumstances.

In the Gospels of both Luke and Matthew, Jesus teaches us how to pray. In The Lord's Prayer, Jesus teaches us to say, "Give us today our daily bread" (Matthew 6:11 and Luke 11:3). Why would Jesus teach us to pray "Give us *today* …"? Why didn't He suggest we pray for enough food (resources) to make it to the next paycheck, or the end of the year, or for the next few generations?! The answer is simple. He's teaching us to pray for what we need *today*. He's teaching us that we can wait until the moment we need something before we can expect it, even if it's food to keep us alive. Talk about patience! He's teaching us that worry, anxiety, and fear about the future are unnecessary. Focus on today. Trust.

As irony would have it, around halfway through typing this chapter about patience, I had a computer glitch that resulted in the loss of much of what I had written. When I realized the work had been lost, my initial reaction could only be described as level 10 frustration. As my blood pressure jumped to life-threatening levels, I saw the cruel irony of the situation. My patience was being tested—while piecing together a chapter outlining the importance of staying cool, calm, and collected. I was certain God was evaluating my mettle—and I almost failed. Instead of hurling my laptop across the room, I decided to slow down, breathe, and think logically. In doing so, I casually researched options for retrieval of my work, thoroughly confident there was no hope. In under two minutes, I had all the work recovered. Patience works.

Small Patience, Big Difference

Steven Spielberg, arguably the most accomplished movie director of all time, made his first home movie when he was twelve. His methods were rudimentary, using the simplest of techniques for "special" effects. In one of his early short films, he had actors slam their foot onto small, slanted boards that would throw dirt up into the air when stepped on, resembling the effects of an explosion. If the scene didn't look right, he would put the board back in place, throw some more dirt on one end, and do a retake.

Unlike movie directors, we don't always get a do-over. We can't go back in time and correct our episodes of impatience. But starting now, we *can* do better. And, like the young Spielberg, we can start small, using what tools we have at our disposal to make big differences.

Each day, we can use the subtle nuisances that we will inevitably face to test ourselves. When you are trying to get in touch with customer service and that annoying, automated "answering service" takes your call, don't take your frustration out on the poor soul who finally does answer. When that associate doesn't text you back, or the short visit to the doctor's office turns into an hour, or the waiter gets your order wrong, or that person takes your parking space, or the line at the coffee shop is too long, or your flight is delayed—breathe. Consider these circumstances opportunities for you to practice, and perfect, the kind of patience that translates into peace. If you cannot apply patience on the small stuff, how can you do so for the big things? If your intolerance has bested you in the past, be ready to slay that dragon of impatience the next time a delay comes.

Divine Delays

Several years ago, Konrad and Jennifer of Burbank, California, were moving their box spring mattress out of their apartment and got stuck on the elevator. After summoning help the couple was finally able to exit and be on their way. Suddenly, they noticed a young boy on a third-floor balcony place his leg over the railing. The toddler, who was autistic, had been joyously throwing toys over the edge onto the ground below and wanted to follow suit. Konrad and Jennifer found themselves rushing to put the mattress under the balcony. A few seconds afterward, the young boy fell, landing directly onto the mattress, completely unscathed (Tchekmedyian 2014).

Sometimes, delays are for a reason. Have persistent faith that you're on your way to fulfilling your purpose in life—and not in spite of these "setbacks," but quite possibly *because* of them. This is part of what makes patience so important. We never know if life's interruptions may be a part of God's master plan. Who knows, we may find ourselves saving a life—or being the one who is saved.

Encouragement

I waited patiently for the Lord; he turned to me and heard my cry.

— Psalm 40:1

God knows that life is hard. He knows that there are times you are tempted to become frustrated and anxious. He knows you struggle—that life hurts, and that you will cry and grieve. He hears you and He loves you. Be patient with Him. Let God work things out in His perfect timing. If you know the final score of a soccer game, would you be on the edge of your seat—concerned your team wasn't going to win—while watching a replay? Of course not, you'd already know the outcome. That's what faith is. It allows us to be patient, knowing that God will supply all our needs. When we learn to be patient with God, it can more easily translate to patience with others… and vice versa.

Ultimately, you'll need to make the decision—the decisive commitment to adopting the rare skill of becoming more patient—if you want to avoid the pitfalls of not doing so. Drop the pacifier. You have the power to wield peace or discontentment, faith or anxiety, trust or fear. My encouragement is that you have what it takes.

The bald eagle, like most animals in the wild, will seek shelter when unfavorable weather comes. However, there are times when a storm approaches so quickly that the eagle doesn't have time to hunt down suitable, protective shelter. At that point, the eagle can fly over the storm, putting itself in a position to *over*come adversity. Learn from the eagle. Rise above the storms we encounter in everyday life. Work to be a more patient spouse, parent, and friend. Have patience with your boss, colleagues, and employees. Be patient with strangers, be patient with yourself. By doing this, you'll be proving your patience with God—and that brings a peace beyond understanding.

CHAPTER 8

INITIATIVE

Thus, although I have heard of reckless haste in war,
I have never seen wise delay.

—*Art of War,* Sun Tzu

The Parking Lot

Driving to Odessa CrossFit that cool afternoon, my mind was on fire. I couldn't focus on traffic, pedestrians, stoplights, or anything else. For all I know I ran every stop sign. I was hypnotized by the video I had watched a few minutes earlier and could not concentrate on anything but pangs of remorse. I was sick to my stomach, consumed by what I can only describe as a holy anger.

But that rage wasn't for my ex-girlfriend or her husband. It was directed at my own reluctance. I stepped out of my pickup and tried to walk but I couldn't; my body wasn't ready to move until my resolve was. I fell to one knee, hidden between two parked cars. At that moment, it was only God and me, and He was waiting for an answer.

Was I going to keep wallowing in indecision, or stop whining and take action?

Battle Bold, LLC

It was October of 2014 when I came across a Facebook post by my college (ex)girlfriend with a news story about her husband who, according to the report, had become a financially successful entrepreneur. I had been longing to own my own business for some time, but had not yet taken the steps to do so. I'm not sure if it was a knee-jerk reaction of pride or envy, but the news of my former inamorata basking in achievement while I seemed stuck with a *wish* did not sit well. In truth, it hurt beyond words.

No matter what part of my insecurity was nudged, God used that video to show me that it was my own pitiful fear of failure that was keeping me from achievement. He used a superficial social media post to draw a line in the sand. I found myself faced with a choice. I could keep complaining about not being given the same opportunities as others, or I could take the talents He had given me and apply them. It was at that moment, cocooned by cars and faced with what seemed like a divine ultimatum, that I made the decision to start my own company.

That evening I jumped on eBay and ordered the only thing I could afford that might kick-start a business: a single-action, hand-operated screen printer for $149. To this day, it's proven to be the most life-altering purchase I have ever made (except for an engagement ring, of course). The next day I elicited my better half (Lauren) to help me come up with a "cool" name for a shirt company. We cycled through dozens of words that resonated with masculinity: "Axe," "Warrior," "Fighter," and other far-too-ridiculous clichés of machismo. Then she said, "How about 'Battle Bold'"?

Honestly, I wasn't a fan at the time. But when your wife says she likes a name, you use it.

For the next several years I worked tirelessly to learn the nuances of business and grow Battle Bold, LLC, while also maintaining a *real* job. I quickly learned that the rumors of entrepreneurship being difficult are very true, especially when you have no idea what you're doing. With no financial backing and no mentor, I was forced to learn business basics the hard way. I climbed a steep learning curve.

In the end, however, it was worth it. I can't possibly articulate the reward—and I don't mean financial. Stepping across that divine line, taking action to transition my wish into a reality taught me the incredible power of *initiative*.

Taking the Initiative

Making the Miracle
Initiative is defined as *the power or opportunity to act or take charge.* Too often, we do not embrace such action as a virtue. Many times, we fail to *take initiative.*

I've heard it said that a goal without a plan is just a wish. And that's what I had, a wish. I was a pitiful dreamer unwilling to act. I was afraid—and disinclined—to learn how to appropriately achieve, and subsequently wasted time and energy worrying while not getting any closer to my dream becoming reality. I did not have enough courage to override my reluctance.

That day in the parking lot was a turning point. It was the moment my God-given entrepreneurial spirit collided with my fear of failure. I had known I wanted to advance, to do something great, but I had a pathetic illusion that my ambition would happen on its own. I was depending on time, luck, and miracles to get me where I wanted to go, waiting for something or someone else. But God does not make us weak. We are made in His image, and to feel we are anything less than authoritative is simply inaccurate. That was my realization. That was the line God drew in front of me. It was my job to take the divine gifts and make the miracle.

Ganas (Desire)

> *Life is a struggle and the potential for failure is ever*
> *present, but those who live in fear of failure, or*
> *hardship, or embarrassment*
> *will never achieve their potential.*

— *Make Your Bed*, William H. McRaven

In early 2018, I had the unique opportunity to sit in on the early stages of a very intriguing selection process. The local city council had agreed to offer aspiring entrepreneurs substantial funding in exchange for the guarantee that their future businesses would open and then operate within city limits. Almost $1 million would be divided between ten motivated, wannabe capitalists. Dozens were chomping at the bit for a cut of the *free* money, all excited about the potential of accessing what I considered to be insane generosity. The city's representative, a short man with a very formal bearing, quietly walked to the front of the room, his thin-framed glasses overlooking his smirk. Once he settled in behind the podium, he did not hesitate to bring the pain: "I've been in this business for a long time. I could fill stadiums, hundreds of them, with the 'ideas' I've heard over the years. I don't care about your ideas; I care about your actions. We will award people not on what they say, but by what they do. If you came here thinking you're going to be given anything, you're wrong."

The air left the room. In an instant, a line revealed itself between those on the receiving end of his unapologetically brazen announcement. The few in the audience who were ready to work, to take the initiative, looked confident—while most everyone else shut down, frozen by the demand for action. That "free" money would only go to those who were willing to work for it, those who had the power to take charge.

Initiative takes both courage and a willingness to work. Just like a dead battery can't power anything, a person without mettle is lacking in prized energy. Unfortunately, far too many people live like dead batteries.

Graveyard Hopes and Cheap Replicas
People waste time and talent by not taking risks. It may be laziness, a lack of inspiration, fear, ignorance, denial, or a mix of it all—but something inhibits them. Although a fire may have burned bright at some point, many people eventually succumb to defeat, duped by the enemy into believing that

they can't accomplish the dreams they hold within. The flame of ambition slowly dims and, ultimately, disappears. It's a tragedy as old as death itself.

> *Why is the graveyard so wealthy? Why is there so*
> *much treasure in the cemetery? Why? Because buried*
> *in the cemetery are dreams that were never fulfilled,*
> *books that were never written, ideas that never became*
> *reality, visions that were never manifested. There in the*
> *graveyard are paintings that were never painted, songs*
> *that were never written...*

—— Dr. Myles Munroe

In some instances, we replace our dreams and ambitions with a cheap substitute—we compromise. Like the tactful thief who carefully removes an invaluable jewel from the mantle and replaces it with a counterfeit replica, we too take our most daring, audacious aspirations and exchange them for a low-value imitation. Though far less rewarding, it's easier that way. And in today's world, it's only getting easier.

Cory Arcangel published a book called *Working on My Novel* that shows tweets from various other "authors." Page after page reveals people, clearly *not* doing so, claiming to be *working on a novel.* They are tweeting about productivity, but the work doesn't seem to be getting done. They are exclaiming to the world that they are getting closer to becoming a bona fide novelist, without actually becoming a bona fide novelist. This is just one example of how people compromise their desires for a cheap substitute. And it happens to the best of us.

In 1934, writer and political activist Upton Sinclair was campaigning to be elected governor of California. In a bizarre effort to garner favor, he wrote a short book *prior* to the election entitled *I, Governor of California, and How I Ended Poverty: A True Story of the Future.* Interestingly, after the book's release, Sinclair showed *less* interest in becoming governor—his enthusiasm for the position tapered. Though it had not become a reality, in his mind he had already experienced life as the governor of California. He had settled for a cheap replica. A year later, he published another book: *I, Candidate for Governor: And How I Got Licked.*

Whether it's tweeting about writing a novel or prematurely living out a fantasy in your mind, compromising our dreams is a common, disheartening charade. When first working on this book, I knew I would be tempted to replace the *invaluable jewel* with a *counterfeit imitation.* At the time, I was very active on Instagram and, when I got honest with myself, knew I would be tempted to post about it—but not *be* about it. I recognized that the surest way for me to not write *It's a Process* was for me to publicly announce my efforts to do so prior to publication. So, when I was really ready to dig in, I deleted Instagram and promised myself to not open it again until I had the book in hand.

> *It's a temptation that exists for everyone—for talk and hype to replace action.*
>
> —— Ryan Holiday, *Ego is the Enemy*

Brian "Tosh" Chontosh

On March 25, 2003, the US invasion of Iraq (Operation Iraqi Freedom) had only been underway for a few days. That morning, a platoon commander named Brian Chontosh was confidently in charge of Weapons Company, 3rd Battalion, 5th Marines, 1st Marines division. After ten years of service, he had thoroughly established himself as a respected leader. That morning, Lieutenant Chontosh climbed into the passenger seat of an armored High Mobility Multipurpose Wheeled Vehicle (HMMWV) and, along with other Marines dispersed in other armored vehicles, moved to spearhead his battalion's mechanized column as it headed north along Route 1 on the way to Baghdad.

All seemed quiet and uneventful. Then, it wasn't. In a swift, coordinated attack, Iraqi forces unleashed a scathing hale of mortars, rocket-propelled grenades, and deadly rounds from multiple machine guns onto his platoon. The Marines had ventured into a well-set trap, a hellacious ambush. Retreating was hopelessly problematic, sitting idly would have meant certain death, and moving forward was not a possibility. The Americans were stuck in what is known as a *kill zone*—sitting ducks with only seconds to live. Death for the Marines seemed inevitable.

Lieutenant Chontosh had no options—so he made one. After noticing a small breech on his flank, he ordered the driver of his HMMWV to charge through it. In doing so, the Marines found themselves face to face with an entrenched machine gunner.

What happened next is nothing short of extraordinary. The formal citation outlines those next moments:

> Without hesitation, First Lieutenant Chontosh ordered the driver to advance directly at the enemy position enabling his .50 caliber machine gunner to silence the enemy. He then directed his driver into the enemy trench, where he exited his vehicle and began to clear the trench with an M16A2 service rifle and 9-millimeter pistol. His ammunition depleted, First Lieutenant Chontosh, with complete disregard for his safety, twice picked up discarded enemy rifles and continued his ferocious attack. When a Marine following him found an enemy rocket propelled grenade launcher, First Lieutenant Chontosh used it to destroy yet another group of enemy soldiers. When his audacious attack ended, he had cleared over 200 meters of the enemy trench, killing more than 20 enemy soldiers and wounding several others (Sterner n.d.).

This incident became known as the "The Ambush" by Chontosh and his fellow Marines—and it's a great example of how courage combined with action can be profoundly effective. *Initiative* was not just a good idea, it was necessary for *survival*. By taking decisive, deliberate action, Lieutenant Chontosh not only saved himself, but also the lives of several fellow Marines, earning him the prestigious Navy Cross. He would continue his military career for another 10 years, including a tour to Fallujah during Operation Phantom Fury.

Interestingly, Chontosh's propensity to take the initiative reaches beyond his military life. After retiring as a major, he would become somewhat of an ultra-athlete; competing in multiple, grueling endurance events around the world, including The Arrowhead 135, a race in northern Minnesota that has been hailed as "one of the 50 toughest races in the world." In 2020, Chontosh recognized a need in the veteran community and created a nonprofit organization, the Big Fish Foundation, dedicated to supporting and mentoring veterans. As if that wasn't enough, as I type this (December, 2022), he is part of a 4-man team dubbed "Shut Up and Row" that is attempting to row a small boat across the Atlantic Ocean to help promote the foundation and its mission. The list goes on.

Tosh is a doer, living out the power of *initiative*—and someone we could all learn from.

Good Things Take Time (and Effort)

When I was young, a "car wash" meant I spent an hour or so investing water, soap, and copious amounts of elbow grease in bringing out the "bright and shiny" on my stepdad's Oldsmobile. Today, that vigorous hour or so is now condensed into a few relaxed minutes as my pickup glides gracefully through a sea of automated brushes.

It seems like each generation is being conditioned to have desires met faster and easier—possibly detrimentally. By cultivating this more/faster mentality, we are tempted to feel that *everything* should come quickly and, in consequence, we reject that which does not. We become lazy, convinced that action is unnecessary for accomplishment. However, some things can *only* be achieved with time and effort. If we reject such requisites—classify them as obsolete—we miss out on the feeling of achievement that is *based* on time and effort. Starting and operating a business, conceptualizing and growing a nonprofit organization, rowing across the Atlantic Ocean, or just writing a book takes patience. *It's a process.*

Yes, we can and should enjoy the technology that makes some aspects of our lives easier and gets things done faster. But we must never allow ourselves to become accustomed to an intolerance of *slow*. We must always be willing to do things that need to be done over and over again, to be ready to take initiative and act over the long haul.

> *The more often he feels without acting,*
> *the less he will be able ever to act, and, in the long run,*
> *the less he will be able to feel*
>
> — *The Screwtape Letters*, C. S. Lewis

Biblical Review

Divine Discernment

We all need courage to live out our God-given purpose. That's what *potential* is: the incredible power within each person that requires audacity to reveal—something we all need to do to move forward. However, it's important to know the difference between moving *forward* and just moving. If you're busy, committed, focused, determined, inspired, tenacious—but not seeking out your God-given purpose— you are spinning your wheels. Like a car in a quagmire, the wheels may be turning, but you're not going anywhere. So how do we know when to act and when to be still? We fervently pray … and then listen.

I will instruct you and teach you in the way you should go; I will counsel you with my loving eye on you.

— Psalm 32:8

There are two tragedies, relative to our goals, that can happen in life. One is not having the courage to move toward them, to be distracted by apathy, depression, bitterness, or anything else that inhibits initiative. The other is using our energy, effort, and gifts to pursue the *wrong* dreams. This is why we need *divine discernment.* It is important to be able to understand what messages are coming from God and what messages are not.

Assessing the root of our desires is a great way to differentiate their source. What are your goals based upon? What inspires your dreams? If it's fame, glory, prestige, wealth, or power, you're gearing up for the wrong battle. Don't let the enemy convince you otherwise. Satan is the most advanced, professional manipulator in existence, and, if you're not careful, he will find a kink in your armor.

For our struggle is not against flesh and blood, but against the rulers, against the authorities, against the powers of this dark world and against the spiritual forces of evil in the heavenly realms.

— Ephesians 6:12

Author Molly Wilcox wrote: "The best way I know how to discern God's voice is to be able to measure my thoughts and attitudes against God's word and to look to scripture to see if what I think I'm hearing from God is God's voice" (Wilcox 2022).

This is exactly what needs to happen. We must first know God's character by reading, studying, and praying. Then, when we feel a stirring in our soul, a desire to move forward, we will be able to recognize whose voice we are hearing. We must listen intently, too, not confusing the source of our motivation. God was the one who called me to start Battle Bold, but He was certainly *not* the one whispering thoughts of infidelity to me at the Devil's River. God isn't going to put a dream in your heart that isn't in His *and* your best interests.

The Porn Star

Several years ago, I met a woman who was, to put it bluntly, a "successful" porn star. Even today, among those in the industry, Brianna (as I'll call her) is one of the most well-known erotic film actresses. She was introduced to me as a friend of a friend and, to my surprise, proved incredibly kind, generous, and thoughtful. Even today, I'm not sure I've met anyone more benevolent. Ironically enough, despite our obvious differences, we became somewhat close (not *that* close). What's interesting about my prurient pal is that she, at the time we met, claimed to be a Christian. Brianna believed that pornography was her *calling*, that her not-so-clad career was the path to her purpose. As we spoke on the issue, I was astounded by her words. She claimed that, even though her body had been subject to unimaginable violations over the years, she was spiritually "untouchable." She was convinced that her inner self was unscathed. Brianna, although a wonderful person in so many ways, was sorely misguided. She was believing a lie—listening to the wrong voice.

This is a great example of how we can trick ourselves. When we become captivated by an inclination, even if we know it's wrong, we have a tendency to twist and manipulate it to align with what we *hope* to be true. Like hammering a square peg in a round hole, we forcefully take our selfish impressions and label them as divinely inspired. Brianna allowed herself to be tricked, fooled into thinking a life of sexual deviance and divine purpose were the same.

No, we may not all be "porn stars," but masking our self-seeking desires as God's purpose for us is equally flawed. When fame, fortune, power, or prestige are possible, it's easy to bury our moral compass or use denial to cover the truth. This is where acting with courage kicks in—the daring to veer away from worldly pursuits and follow the wiser voice. Fighting the world is dauntingly arduous—and fighting yourself is even more so.

Fight anyway.

Let us not become weary in doing good, for at the proper time we will reap a harvest if we do not give up.

— Galatians 6:9

Stay Battle Ready

Having the *courage* to act, to take the initiative based on what God reveals to us, is not always a smooth ride. Those who want *easy* will need to change their mindset before following the teachings of Christ. Jesus said: "I am sending you out like sheep among wolves." (Matthew 10:16) Does that sound like a comfortable life? It's not. In fact, it's often a call to arms. You think Satan wants you to fulfill your *divine* calling? That he wants you to do anything *but* ignore or deny God? If you want to act on what God tells you, be ready for the fight of your life.

> *Therefore put on the full armor of God, so that when the day of evil comes, you may be able to stand your ground, and after you have done everything, to stand.*
>
> —— Ephesians 6:13

In early November of 1938, what would become known as *Kristallnacht* (German, "Crystal Night" or "night of broken glass") took place throughout Germany, Austria, and the Sudetenland. It was a coordinated attack by the Nazis, who severely damaged synagogues, stores, homes, hospitals, and schools that were part of Jewish communities. They mercilessly swept through cities—breaking, burning, looting, and ransacking. Over the following weeks, many of the already victimized Jews were arrested, incarcerated, and/or deported to concentration camps, from which they would never return. However, it was not just the *action* that was so devastating in those tumultuous times, but the *inaction* as well. It's well-known that many local Germans who witnessed the attacks did not act against the Nazi perpetrators, even though they later claimed to have opposed the violence. During *Kristallnacht*, they were disgusted by what they witnessed, but were too afraid to act.

Again, initiative takes courage.

Possibility of Failure

One reason people fail to act is because of the risk that is often involved. Whether you're trapped in a Kill Zone surrounded by an enemy, working against your own selfish desires, standing up to a fascist regime, or just trying to start your own business, there is a chance of failure. Even when we are certain that we're listening to and acting on divine directives, it may not always pan out like we hoped. But that's part of the deal. Paul teaches us that we may not always rule the day.

> *Whoever digs a pit may fall into it;*
> *whoever breaks through a wall may be*
> *bitten by a snake.*

— Ecclesiastes 10:8

Yes, opening a business may result in you being drenched in debt with nothing to show for it. Quitting your job to pursue another may leave you unemployed. Packing up your belongings and moving across the country may result in solitude, possibly even homelessness. Standing up for the bullied may leave you with a black eye, or worse. But risk is part of it—and God's ways are not our ways. Remember, heeding divine discernment means you are going to war. If

God is nudging you to act, do it. When it's time to move, move—and let the chips fall where they may.

But someone will say, 'You have faith; I have deeds.'
Show me your faith without deeds, and I will show you
my faith by my deeds

— James 2:18

The Solution

Audentes Fortuna Iuvat

The ancient Roman poet Publius Vergilius Maro (Virgil) wrote "*audentes fortuna iuvat,*" which translates to *fortune favors the bold.* He's not wrong. Prosperity indeed has a tendency to attach to those with the courage to take risks. However, being "bold" doesn't always mean having a *kill-or-be-killed* mentality. Don't think of boldness as running at an enemy swinging an axe while screaming a battle cry. Sometimes it simply means having the nerve to do what's right when others don't.

Being honest, when doing so doesn't seem advantageous, is courageous. Offering kindness to someone who we don't feel deserves it is daring, and working diligently when no one is watching reveals mettle. Apologizing for something you did not do in order to keep the peace is *bold.* Then again, sometimes we will need to dash forward with a battle axe.

Warren Buffett, chairman and CEO of Berkshire Hathaway—one of the wealthiest men in the world—has cited *The Intelligent Investor* as one of the best books on investing ever written. In it are several principles for successful investing. The fourth reads, "If you have formed a conclusion from the facts and if you know your judgement is sound, *act on it*—even though others may hesitate or differ" (Graham 2005).

In other words, when it comes time to move … move. And never mind what anyone else says. Don't sit. Don't ponder. Don't assess cost or risk. Don't get trapped in a cycle of endless analyzing or deliberating. Don't hesitate. When He speaks, drop the cowardice.

Go!

Meeting God Halfway

Where the Red Fern Grows is a 1974 film that I first saw when I was very young. There's a scene in which the main character, twelve-year-old Billy Coleman, wants nothing more than to own his own coon-hunting dogs. Unfortunately, he's far too poor to buy anything, much less a pair of quality K-9s. After witnessing a rude, unappreciative family take away the dog of his dreams, Billy laments with his wise grandfather.

Billy: "I don't know, Grandpa. Sometimes I don't think God wants me to have any."

Grandpa: "Now, why do you say a thing like that?"

Billy: "Well, I've been asking him for dogs as long as I can remember and nothin's happened yet."

Grandpa: "Maybe you haven't done your fair share."

Billy: "What do you mean?"

Grandpa: "Well, it's been my experience *God helps those who help themselves.* Now, don't get me wrong. If God wanted to, he could give you hounds as easy as cuttin' lard. But that wouldn't do much for your character."

Billy: "I don't want character. I want dogs!"

Grandpa: "And if you want them bad enough, you'll get them, Billy. And if you want God's help bad enough, *you'll meet Him halfway.*"

Meeting God "halfway" is something that has stuck with me, and it's something we are all called to do.

Joel Osteen is the senior pastor of Lakewood Church in Houston, Texas. He's often accused of preaching the *prosperity gospel,* the belief that God's will for devout Christians is material gain. Having a net worth of more than $50 million, he is often demonized for living with extravagant wealth (Burton 2017). I don't care to argue either way about his preaching style, but I do want to point out his willingness to go *halfway*—his commitment to initiative. As of late 2022, Pastor Osteen has written 21 books and preached over 1,000 sermons. Before he became the leader of Lakewood Church, he worked for 17 years producing his father's televised sermons. He has worked, hard.

When you are willing to meet God halfway, you will get to where God wants you—you might even find yourself *prosperous.* But that's not the point. Meeting God halfway isn't about trying to obtain your favorite coon dog or becoming a multi-millionaire. It's about taking action, using your God-given gifts and aligning your intent with His. It's about putting in the effort to walk the divine path outlined for each one of us—the one no one else on earth can take.

You can't climb a mountain sitting on your ass—go meet God halfway.

Burn the Ships

In 1519, Hernán Cortés arrived in what is now Mexico as one of the first Spanish explorers of the New World. Soon after landing, the grumblings and whispers among his men began. They were uncomfortable and afraid, and wanted to return to Spain. However, Cortés wasn't about tucking tail and heading home—and he knew that as long as the dozen or so ships sat on the beach, his men would be distracted. So, what did Cortés do? He had his men, many of whom were hoping to return home, destroy their only chance of doing so. He told them to *burn the ships*.

Every day, every moment, you and I have a choice. We can become distracted, lured away from what is best for us—or not. We can climb the not-so-comfortable mountain that is, ironically enough, leading our best life—or we can sit idly, without courage, unwilling to move. It's important that each of us carefully consider what is distracting us from taking the appropriate initiative. For me, completely severing my involvement with social media was the only way I could concentrate on writing *It's a Process*. Instagram was far too great a temptation for me to adequately study, meditate, pray, and work. I simply could not do both. For a long time, I tried to justify trying that approach.

Instagram has pictures of my children! Facebook is the only way I can stay in touch with those who would otherwise be long-*lost* friends! I can't cut them out of my life—that would be rude and irresponsible! Eventually, though, I had to face the truth. Although it was difficult, I deleted Instagram from my phone—confirming to myself that I would return only after the book was complete.

What is distracting you? What is luring you away from what you know you *should* be doing? What lies have you told yourself about what's actually necessary and what can wait? Social media? Your television? A video game? Alcohol? Tobacco? Pills? Drugs? Pornography? Something else?!

Stop. Pray. Listen. Be honest with yourself and identify the distraction, then have the *courage* to act on it. Take the initiative and, like a surgeon removing a cancerous mass, cut out whatever it is. So much of what distracts us is so small and insignificant relative to the life of peace God has for us.

Burn the ships.

Encouragement

I heard a pastor once say, "You and God are a majority." He's right. There's nothing that can keep you from achieving whatever God has put in your heart and mind if you have the courage to fight. Whatever you feel called to do, whatever God is whispering in your soul—*move.*

I hope you never find yourself tucked between two parked cars, defeated by the sense of failure. I hope you never find yourself in a kill zone or paralyzed by fear. I hope that you never have a problem with a lack of courage or a breakdown of initiative. Most importantly, I hope you never fail to read and heed God's word about how capable you are. But if you do, there is good news. You have what it takes to do better. You have what it takes to act—to take the fight to whatever is holding you back. You are not a cowardly lion. You're a God-made, devil-crushing, dream-catching, divinely-guided, badass fighter who is ready to go to war against any doubt, person, idea, company, or society that separates you from what you are called to do. Be patient, but not passive.

Take the initiative.

Audentes Fortuna Iuvat

CHAPTER 9

OWNERSHIP

Amateurs blame others.
Professionals accept responsibility.

— Shane Parrish

Tyson the Terminator

"Can you meet me in the conference room for a second?" he asked, as his tall, thin frame breezed across my office doorway.

Tyson, my supervisor, was usually kind and cheerful. In the two years we had worked together, I had never once seen him angry or unstable. Even after I asked the same question four times in a row, struggling to understand the nuances of crude oil marketing, Tyson seemed infinitely understanding. He was half my age yet incredibly intelligent. However, today he was more direct than usual. I sensed a nervousness too. Tyson continued down the hallway toward the conference room.

"It's time," I thought to myself.

I had been in this situation before—and I recognized my gut-wrenching conjecture. I rose from my desk and made my way down the hallway, the same corridor that just days before had hosted Tyson and me playing a friendly round of "office golf."

As I entered the small, eight-chair conference room, Tyson was seated next to a somber-looking woman I didn't recognize. My hand flinched upward for an introductory handshake. I smiled, but she didn't look up. I knew. I had just walked the office version of *The Green Mile*. My hand fell back into place as I sat across from them, both emotionless.

Tyson spoke softly, barely above a whisper.

"I hope you know I respect you as a person; more than anything I value you as a friend, which makes this even more difficult. But we're gonna have to let you go."

Even if a man knows that the bite is inevitable, it doesn't hurt any less. Tyson hung his head and walked out the door, leaving me alone with the woman who would explain the details of my termination—a condemned man being read his last rights.

I spent the next few minutes boxing up my various personal belongings: the painting my daughter made, the toy car my son had given me, other little office mementos, and a new book I had recently purchased but hadn't yet read. Looking back, if I had opened that book earlier, there's a good chance Tyson would have never called me into the conference room.

Extreme Ownership

Launching upward, I sat up with such force that the bed's heavy wooden frame shuddered violently. The words were screaming at me, as if they had been trying to get my attention for decades. Buried in that book was a treasure I didn't know I was looking for—and it was magnificent.

I read it again.

> *Total responsibility for failure is a difficult thing to accept, and taking ownership when things go wrong requires extraordinary humility and courage. But doing just that is an absolute necessity to learning ...*

—— Extreme Ownership

God was in those words.

It was a divine sledgehammer—a hit to my soul that literally made me nauseous. I was instantly drowning in a paradoxical epiphany of both regret and euphoria. I was 42 years old, a father of two, and unemployed after being terminated for the fourth time in my adult life—and yet, for the first time, I knew exactly why I was perpetually failing. God let me realize the truth about why I was in the situation I was in. I was enraged, unable to turn my eyes from the pages. I had been doing it all wrong.

"Why did you not show this to me earlier!?" I bellowed, my voice echoing through the empty house.

I felt His response immediately, a clear answer as to why it took so long. I had not been exposed to the truth of what the real problem was for one simple reason: up to that point, I would not have been willing to accept the responsibility. I would not have believed that I was to blame. For the lesson to take hold, my ego had to have been completely eradicated. Like rotten flesh must be thoroughly excised for restoration to happen, every hint of pride needed to be cut away from my character before healing—which required humility—could take place. I had to be shattered before I could understand that, of all the failures I had endured, pointing the finger at anyone but the person looking back at me from the mirror was incorrect. I was the problem.

I was sitting alone in bed, just three weeks after being fired, and I could clearly see how the decisions *I had made* led me to that point. For years I had pointed the finger at others. To validate my failures, I had labeled people in my life as arrogant, pompous, and manipulative. But it was actually me that I had been describing; I was the one with the character flaw. The Isaacs of life were not to blame, the Coach Bookers weren't at fault either. It wasn't the bullies, stepdads, business owners, supervisors, co-workers, or anyone else who was liable for *my* actions and *my* disappointments. I had been living through the same, tired movie for years—having the wrong attitude, throwing a pity party, ending up without direction, and casting blame on someone or something else.

But that day, it stopped. That day, I took ownership.

Ownership: It's on You

Developing Resilience

Too often we find ourselves passing the buck. We point the finger at just about every person, place, or thing as a default response to a less-than-favorable situation. We blame teachers when our children don't get good grades. We blame coaches when our kid doesn't play. We blame city leaders for increases in crime, politicians for botched policy, or the "psycho ex" for a failed relationship. Blame is in our blood.

We're doing it wrong.

Faulting others for failures only contributes to their prevalence. At the very least, it robs us of an opportunity. If we perpetually believe we are innocent, not to blame for something that has gone wrong, we won't take the action needed to avoid another, similar disappointment. We miss the chance to change. Of course, taking ownership is not a path to preventing *all* failure, but it is a healthy way to put it in the proper perspective, to see our botched moments as something that we can learn from. When we realize that it's not *life* that knocks us down, but ourselves, we can work to become more resilient. If we do not develop the resiliency that comes with ownership, we will continue to be broken by our ignorance.

Better Late Than Never

> *If you have tried it, leave it, I repeat,*
> *Lest you lose all; better than never is late.*

—*The Canon's Yeoman's Tale,* Geoffrey Chaucer

It's embarrassing—the tattered road of failures that comprise my resume. But, as they say, it's better late than never. I only wish I had seen it sooner!

The heavy metal rock singer Marilyn Manson wrote, "You can't see the forest for the trees. You can't smell your own shit on your knees" (Lyrics.com 2022). That was me, alone in the forest of ignorance and denial, constantly accusing others of sabotage and unable to see the real problem—a habit that carried heavy consequences. Between the ages of 33 and 43, I had eight different "careers," most of which ended in bitterness. After each termination or resignation, I targeted someone else—usually the boss. You would think that after a time or two, I would have been able to identify the root cause. In retrospect, it's hard to imagine how I could not recognize the common denominator. But the forest was dense, and I was proud. I wasn't willing to be honest with myself and make an unbiased consideration of the *actual* problem.

> *We do not learn from experience ...*
> *we learn from reflecting on experience.*

— John Dewey

To constantly claim victimization is much easier than bearing the burden of personal liability. There is much less effort in accusation than in accountability. That's why we are so quick to deflect responsibility—but this is self-constricting. A habit of casting blame on others, averting what should be directed toward the self, results in only heartache. When we perpetually claim to be manipulated, we are only manipulating ourselves.

For years I failed to see it. Like a toddler who can't reach the top shelf, I was not yet mature enough to reach the truth of my serial errors. It wasn't until God used *Extreme Ownership* to send a very clear message ... one which He couldn't send until I was defeated enough to be receptive. I learned the value of accountability the hard way.

Accountability, Respect, and Cohesion

We can't solve problems by using the same kind of thinking we used when we created them.

— Albert Einstein

If you want to make friends, don't blame them. When someone feels like they're constantly in the crosshairs of an irrational colleague who throws darts of accusation, conflict will be ever-present. The allegations will find their target, and the victims won't respond well. You cannot perpetually accuse others of being at fault and logically expect them to collaborate with you. This truth spans the workforce all the way down to the kindergarten playground. Blaming doesn't make buddies. Someone who practices accountability, however, will take a very different approach when something doesn't go right. They will first look to themselves, reflect on what they could have done better, and absorb rational responsibility. Such a response will not go unnoticed. Others will appreciate it.

A person who withholds a prideful rebuke will gain respect, which is the foundation on which quality relationships are forged. Self-accountability fends off discord and promotes cohesion and teamwork. This is important for us to understand if we expect to work (or play) well with others. Pricks don't make the best pals. Ownership yields respect, and respect yields unity. The shadow of ego is dissension, but admiration follows those who hold themselves responsible.

Control: The Last Freedom

The problem with redirecting blame is just that: it's a habit of deflecting *outward*. It points away, pushing fault onto others while discounting one's own responsibility. However, to fix the problem, an *inward* focus must happen. If the ailments of irresponsibility are to be neutralized, the periscope of judgment must be transformed into a microscope of self-analysis. We must look *into* the mirror before looking *out* of the window. But for such a transition to take place, a person must first learn self-control.

And that's exactly what ownership is—control.

To condemn without self-reflection is to relinquish self-control. It's to live as though our lives are subject to the will of others. A person must recognize and harness their own power of influence if they want independence from external forces. In other words, a person can't always play the victim and be fully aware of their own capability at the same time. All people have the incredible power of self-control. But having a defeated, "the world is out to get me" mindset is giving away that power. It's an affirmation that others govern us, as if we are puppets on a string being tossed about at the whim of another. If we feel that others are always to blame, then we are not adequately managing our situation.

Too often we don't recognize the degree to which we govern our circumstances. I'm not talking about humility or modesty. Ownership isn't about being a pushover. It is quite the opposite. It's about strength—the influence and power over ourselves in any situation. No matter how bad things get, no matter how targeted, a person always has power over their perspective. It's the last freedom, the only thing that cannot be taken. It's important to remember this when embracing the ownership mindset.

> *We who lived in concentration camps can remember the men who walked through the huts comforting others, giving away their last piece of bread. They may have been few in number, but they offer sufficient proof that everything can be taken from a man but one thing: that last of human freedoms—to choose one's attitude in any given set of circumstances, to choose one's own way.*

> —— *Man's Search for Meaning*, Viktor E. Frankl

Biblical Review

No Excuse

You may recall the fascinating story in the Gospel of John
about an interaction between Jesus and a crippled man
(mentioned in Chapter 4). As the story goes, Jesus and a small
group of followers found themselves at the Pool of Bethesda,
a region in Jerusalem at which several misfortunate souls
congregated—including the disabled. Many there believed
that the water at the pool had healing powers, so they would
adamantly wait to experience the "stir" of the water.

> *Some time later, Jesus went up to Jerusalem for one of
> the Jewish festivals. Now there is in Jerusalem near
> the Sheep Gate a pool, which in Aramaic is called
> Bethesda and which is surrounded by five covered
> colonnades. Here a great number of disabled people
> used to lie—the blind, the lame, the paralyzed. One
> who was there had been an invalid for thirty-eight
> years. When Jesus saw him lying there and learned
> that he had been in this condition for a long time, he
> asked him, 'Do you want to get well?'*
> *'Sir,' the invalid replied, 'I have no one to help me into
> the pool when the water is stirred. While I am trying
> to get in, someone else goes down ahead of me.'*
> *Then Jesus said to him, 'Get up! Pick up your mat
> and walk.'*

— John 5:1-8

Although there's much to be extracted from the story, I want to emphasize what happened when the crippled man made an excuse. He (the "invalid") redirected blame regarding his inability to get to the water. He claimed that *no one would help him*, that others were at fault. He refused to take ownership. How did Jesus respond? He *ignored* the excuse! Jesus paid no attention whatsoever to the justification and instead told the man, "Get up! Pick up your mat and walk." Which he did!

Jesus cared so little about the crippled man's excuse that He disregarded it completely. Instead, He told the man to *take action*. Buried in this story is the crux, the key point of what ownership is. It's refusing to fault others. We are called to pick up our mat, to get up, and to walk. We are not called to accuse others or whine when things do not go our way. We are certainly *not* called to blame others.

Let's look at another verse, this time from Paul's letter to his church friends of ancient Galatia.

> *Carry each other's burdens, and in this way you will fulfill the law of Christ. If anyone thinks they are something when they are not, they deceive themselves. Each one should test their own actions. Then they can take pride in themselves alone, without comparing themselves to someone else, <u>for each one should carry their own load.</u>*

— Galatians 6:2-5

We are all encouraged to show compassion by helping those in need (Chapter 2). This is very difficult, however, if we refuse to embrace the responsibility of carrying our own load. If we cannot take charge for ourselves, how can we expect to responsibly *carry each other's burdens*? Pointing fingers at others for our failures is not Christ-like accountability. We will not be able to follow the path God has outlined for us if we're constantly complaining and redirecting blame.

We have been blessed with immense authority. To deny responsibility is to squander that power.

The Solution

Ownership and Forgiveness

> *It's not an easy journey, to get to a place where you forgive people. But it is such a powerful place because it frees you.*
>
> —— Tyler Perry

When piecing together *It's a Process*, I considered adding a chapter about the art of forgiveness. After all, it is one of the most important practices a person can adopt if they intend on living life to the fullest. It's hard to move forward when chained to the boulder of bitterness. However, it is sometimes challenging to muster up the humility, courage, and wisdom to forgive. Letting go of animosity is not always the easiest thing to do, as it requires suppression of the ego.

However, for me, an incredible transformation took place when I learned the power of ownership. Once I embraced taking accountability for my failures, those I had held responsible were automatically released. The resentment that was engrained within me disappeared when I realized that most of the errors on my permanent record were of my own doing. When I understood that my former misfortune was a result of my own handiwork, harboring animosity became unnecessary. Furthermore, I realized that in some cases, I was the one that owed someone an apology, since I had wrongfully blamed others for my errors. Taking ownership took many of my circumstances and flipped them upside down. It wasn't particularly enjoyable to admit fault and offer apologies, but shedding the heavy weight of resentment proved a comforting relief. I was able to bear the load of ownership—which proved much easier to manage than the burden of bitterness.

This is just another superpower that comes with assuming responsibility. When you embrace ownership, forgiveness comes easy and humility is abundant.

There is divine power in self-accountability.

Ownership Is Leadership, Leadership Is Ownership

Experience is a master teacher,
even when it's not our own.

— Gina Greenlee

My senior year of high school I ran for student council president—and won. I was nowhere near the ideal candidate, but it helps when kind people nonetheless offer their vote. My classmates—Robert, Shane, Clayton, and Stacey—were all on the council as well, each far more suited to serve as the president. I had not yet matured in many ways, and, in retrospect, it was an opportunity that I regrettably wasted. I chose to brush off the responsibility of learning how to effectively lead and ignorantly passed up on the chance to potentially discover the power of ownership. However, one does not need to be promoted or elected to become a leader—we are leading in ways we may not even recognize.

In some form or fashion, we are setting an example, sending both verbal and nonverbal messages about various aspects of life. However, not all leadership is helpful or effective. Those who constantly complain, bicker, promote discord, and blame are also leaders—just sucky ones. They're leading suboptimally, sending destructive messages which guide people in the wrong direction. In contrast, a person who transitions to a life of *ownership* inevitably shifts to a life of *effective* leadership. One follows the other. A person who exemplifies accountability will, by default, lead by setting a *proper* example. Ownership is the first step to leading both ourselves, and others, with excellence. Once these habits of intent accountability *and* leadership are adopted, a spiral occurs—ownership develops leadership, leadership develops ownership.

The Difficult Team Member

A few years ago, I began working as a manager for a safety company in Odessa, TX. My role was relatively straightforward: coordinate the sales team, which typically numbered between five to ten people. As such, I often worked concurrently with several dynamic, outgoing personalities. I remember one young lady on my team, I'll call her Karen, who was incredibly unique. She was beautiful and cunning, the type of woman you would expect to see depicted in the latest Hollywood movie across from Chris Hemsworth. However, Karen had more than aesthetics and wit, she had an insatiable thirst for dissension. She seemed utterly hellbent on constantly sowing discord among any and all members of the company—a mission rooted in her towering ego. She was also, like Isaac (Chapter 1), an absolute ninja when it came to lying. Instead of using her talents to become a productive part of the team, Karen embraced destructive manipulation, often orchestrating entire departments to become hostile toward one another.

As her manager, it was a challenge, to say the least. Multiple times I would be called to my boss's office and listen as Karen made false accusations toward me (and others). Thankfully, that was after I had been exposed to *Extreme Ownership*, so I was prepared for the Karens of life. I took those otherwise rage-worthy opportunities to better myself. I considered each run-in with her to be a character assessment, a way to measure my mettle of accountability and self-control. I did not pass every test, sometimes allowing my defensiveness to show. But I did learn a lot—and I'm a better leader for it. This is what we all must do. We need to understand everyday frustrations to be quizzes that, if we pass, will help us take control of ourselves.

Get Used to Different

> *The person who follows the crowd will usually go no further than the crowd.*
> *The person who walks alone is likely to find himself in places no one has ever seen before.*

— Albert Einstein

So many people claw their way through life while blinded by a lack of self-responsibility—only to then find themselves in a hole of their own creation. The terrifying epidemics of drug addiction, alcoholism, imprisonment, abuse, unemployment, and even general discontent stem, in large part, from a lack of accountability. Be wise enough to make a change before then. Don't wait until you are broken, beaten, and defeated enough to be receptive to an ownership mindset. Be humble and wise enough to learn early. Learn from my experience. But know this, if you do so, you may find yourself in a league all your own—a lonely one.

Just like so many other lessons outlined in *It's a Process*, not everyone in your life will embrace ownership and, therefore, may not be inclined to accept you. Do you think that many people *want* to consider themselves the culprit instigating their problems? Most do not. In fact, some people may attempt to capitalize on your tendency to take ownership by pouring their failures onto you. Continually taking

196

accountability will make you a target for those who would rather find a scapegoat for their failures. If you are willing to first blame yourself, be ready for others to follow suit.

But that's ok.

A sincere effort to take ownership may isolate you from the herd. You may find yourself on your own. That's what an effective leader sometimes endures. The willingness to be ostracized is part of what makes a great leader. You will be a lone wolf. But this is necessary, it's the mentality you need to take you to places others will never reach. This is what it means to be different—to be exclusive.

Seeking Criticism

> *With Extreme Ownership, you must remove individual ego and personal agenda.*
>
> — Extreme Ownership

As you can tell, I am an unabashed fan of *Extreme Ownership: How U.S. Navy SEALs Lead and Win* by Jocko Willink and Leif Babin. I encourage you to read, study, and apply the lessons outlined in it. However, these cannot take effect if you are not ready. A single drop of pompousness will prevent the monsoon of wisdom captured within its pages from being recognized. Too much ego leaves no room for critical feedback to be appreciated. Of course, it also takes an absence of ego to *encourage* criticism.

Taking ownership means seeking guidance. Whether it is asking fellow leaders to share secrets or simply assessing others to better understand how to improve, "extreme" ownership means taking full responsibility for not only how we behave, but how we can do better. We must constantly seek out wisdom, counsel, and alternative perspectives—and then discern as needed. And therein lies the delicate balance of implementation. If we adopt a new habit in hopes of improving and it doesn't work out, we must accept responsibility and move on. If we miss out on an opportunity to learn, we need to take ownership and do better the next time. Either way, it's on us. Ownership means taking responsibility for the bad advice you did take *and* accepting accountability for the good advice you did not heed.

Encouragement

Why, you do not even know what will happen tomorrow. What is your life? You are a mist that appears for a little while and then vanishes.

—— James 4:14

Make no mistake, our life here on earth is like a mist in the air—it's fleeting. There's nothing we can do to stop the inevitability of our evaporating. However, this doesn't mean we were designed to be *gone with the wind*. We must understand the control we have in our short time on earth and assertively use such to be the person we have been gifted and called to be.

You have power and purpose. You have God-given control, including that which you choose to take ownership of… or don't. Make a habit of looking inward. When bad things happen—when life gets dirty—default to self-reflection. Always put yourself in the interrogator's seat first.

Ask these accountability questions:

What could I have done different?
Is my ego getting in the way?
How can I improve the situation?
<u>*Can I have a better attitude?*</u>

Of course, you can only take ownership of yourself. That's why it's called <u>own</u>ership. But that means you can control, at least in part, *every single situation* you are involved in. You can always control you—so do it.

Carrying the load of your own misfortunes is lesser a burden than carrying the stones of accusation.

CHAPTER 10

FAITH

I sought the Lord, and he answered me;
he delivered me from all my fears.

— Psalm 34:4

The Demon

The usual faint rush of water from the nearby bathroom shower spurred me from a deep sleep, per the norm. Lauren taught second grade in the nearby town of Hearne, and getting our infant daughter to daycare before school required her to rise early. I would typically steal another half hour in bed before beginning my day as a PhD candidate at Texas A&M University. It was a predictable, everyday morning in our young marriage.

Then, all *hell* broke loose.

I was usually in snooze mode while Lauren showered, taking advantage of her absence to stretch across the breadth of our bed. That morning, as I rolled over and dropped my arm over toward her side of the bed—fully expecting to feel nothing but more bed—my hand brushed her shoulder. She was sitting up. I was confused. Her presence was strange. I could clearly hear the water in the adjacent bathroom. Why would she be sitting in bed with the shower running? I was curious—but not enough to open my eyes. Playfully, I moved my hand upward to caress her cheek, but I did not feel the soft contour of her face, but instead something featureless with no mouth, no nose, no eyes—nothing. It felt like a blank, leather canvas where a face *should* be.

Instantly, terror overwhelmed me. I was suddenly awake and alert. But, before I could pull my hand away, a small mouth formed in the bare "face" and bit down hard on the end of my ring finger. It wasn't sharp, but it hurt nonetheless. I yanked my arm from whatever it was, falling onto my back. I desperately tried to open my eyes, to scream, to fight—but nothing worked. I could not move, see, or speak. It was as if my entire body was under a spell, nothing but my indescribable horror was functioning … and at full capacity. Suddenly, I felt something heavy fall on my chest, as if whatever was there had jumped on top of me. It burned, like a lump of hot coal resting on my sternum. I was helplessly immobilized, pinned against the bed. Whatever this was, it had full, unhindered control over me. The fear I felt cannot be articulated with words. Then, abruptly—as quickly as it started—it was gone. In an instant, the pressure on my chest released and I regained control of my body. I shot upward, eyes wide as I gasped for air. I was panicked but ready for a fight. I threw my hand to my heart—my chest still warm. I looked at my finger—the pain of the bite still very real. I desperately scanned the room trying to find whatever evil had attacked me. But there was nothing, just an empty room. Whatever it was, it was gone.

Belief, Not Faith

This incident, which I don't necessarily enjoy sharing, brought with it its own form of trauma. As I type this, only a handful of people know about it, an ignorance shared even by those closest to me. That morning I experienced a horror I never want to relive. However, something good did come from it. I was *aware*. A close encounter with a spiritual force, albeit an unpleasant one, made it very clear that there *are* powerful forces in the unseen realm. My belief in God, demons, and spiritual forces was bolstered to new levels. After such a real, tactile experience, there was no chance I could have been persuaded otherwise.

However, *belief* and *faith* are not the same—something I would learn the hard way.

Only Faith

Belief Isn't Enough

Belief doesn't matter if it's not accompanied by faith. Many people are lacking the latter.

The attack by the demon (or whatever it was) instilled within me a firm *belief* in the unseen. I was certain, beyond any doubt, of the existence of God and spiritual forces. However, belief isn't all that extraordinary. The demons themselves "believe" in God (James 2:19). It's *trust* that matters—and although I had experienced an irrefutable encounter with a terrifying spiritual force, long-term trust in God was still something I didn't fully embrace. It was easy to believe in God, and in the weeks following the attack, I trusted that He was protecting my family. But just like water erodes stone, I would let my dark habits eat away at my <u>trust</u> in Him. Slowly, surely, my faith began to fade.

Most of the struggles outlined in this book stemmed from my unwillingness to fully rely on God. I had belief, but not *faith*. I didn't *trust* in His plan for my life. Instead, I chose to forge my own path, to ignore the divine winds and work tirelessly *against* God. I lived a paradox, claiming to be a Christian while simultaneously trying to create my own fate—and those two things don't work together. It's hypocritical to proclaim that God *has the wheel* while continuing to hold onto it—only one can do the steering. It was a contradiction that led to diminished self-esteem, arrogance, disdain, impatience, and a habitual tendency to blame others. I lived in a constant state of worry, afraid that I wasn't accomplishing enough, fast enough—all because I would not let go.

Belief is only at the fringes of faith—trust is at its core. I only wish I had found the comfort, peace, patience, and wisdom that comes from offering an unrestrained trust in Him earlier.

Our Path

It's not just me. Without trust that we are loved and protected, many people find themselves working ferociously to earn *love* and *protection*. Without an assurance that a divine path has been outlined for each one of us, many spend their lives arduously carving out a trail through the dense forest of life, one they think will lead to peace. They strenuously work and toil alone because they believe they will get to a point at which chopping, hacking, and digging are no longer needed. The problem is, when we attempt to become the fearless, independent pioneer hell-bent on creating our own fate, we put ourselves at risk of being snared. Dishonesty, selfishness, depression, narcissism, hate, intolerance, laziness, and frustration all become pits we can fall into during our insatiable searching. Trekking the forest of life alone is dangerous—and unnecessary. Living with a trust that a loving God has already cleared a path for each of us yields the tranquility we are so desperately trying to find. Faith that a divine direction is readily available is the first step *on* that path.

> *Seek His will in all you do, and he will show you which path to take.*

— Proverbs 3:6

Biblical Review

Transformers

The Apostle Paul outlines the phenomenal transformation that *can* take place in each of us, one that will lead us to the place we're all hoping for. He first describes our lives *before* the alteration, when we are walking alone. Prior to forging a relationship with Christ, Paul says we are following "the ways of this world" (Ephesians 2:2) and are led by "cravings of our flesh" (Ephesians 2:3). He references those who have yet to trust in Him as "deserving of wrath" (Ephesians 2:3) and "dead in transgressions" (2:5).

Talk about a hardcore way to describe life! But this is our condition without faith. Without God, we are puppets of the world, manipulated by the indignant and sinful—unable to follow His plan for our lives. We use what the world defines as success and combine it with our selfish desires to viciously pursue achievement. We are a forester with no bearings, ill-equipped to survive in such a hostile environment. However, something that is "dead" has no purpose in life. To find meaning, we must renovate our way of thinking. We must transform. And Paul teaches us how this transformation can take place:

> *For it is by grace you have been saved, through faith—and this is not from yourselves, if is the gift of God.*

— Ephesians 2:8

Like a rat on a running wheel, our efforts to find peace and purpose without faith and trust in Christ are futile. To genuinely rid ourselves of destructive tendencies, it is not enough to just suppress them. They must be *replaced* by the love, joy, peace, forbearance, kindness, and goodness that comes from Christ (Galatians 5:22-23). As a caterpillar transforms into a butterfly, so too must we transition into a new being if we want to find and follow our divine path. However, unlike the caterpillar, each of us will find ourselves transforming into something different from our neighbor. We are each unique, with a separate and distinctive purpose. We are not all meant to be butterflies.

Body of Christ

*He's not going to ask us how many trophies and
awards we received; He's going to ask us how we used
our gifts to build the body of Christ.*

— Tessa Emily Hall

Years ago, I started a podcast called *How to be 40* in which I articulated my "attempt to delineate what it means to transition from juvenile thinking and behavior to genuine maturity." For over two years, every episode I recorded was just me—sharing my thoughts and perspectives on various aspects of life. However, that all changed when my daughter came back from church camp. McKinlee was fourteen at the time and, after hearing her elaborate on what she had learned there, I begged her to be my first podcast guest—to which she hesitantly agreed. While recording, she revealed a wisdom that legitimately shocked me. She taught me about the "Body of Christ"—how we all have different callings. I realized that my problem of comparison, which had haunted me for decades, stemmed from the idea that we are all running the same race. But as McKinlee pointed out, although we should believe in "one hope," "one Lord," and "one Faith" (Ephesians 4:4-5), we all have our own exclusive divine purpose. Yes, we are all called to trust the Lord to lead us, but we're not all led in the same direction. Unity does not mean *uniformity*.

Oh, how I wish I had embraced such wise words in my youth!

Then we will no longer be infants, tossed back and
forth by the waves,
and blown here and there by every wind of teaching
and by the cunning and craftiness of people in their
deceitful scheming.

—— Ephesians 4:14

Before Christ, when we're living on our own, being "blown here and there by every wind of teaching," we are *lost*. When we rely on our own understanding, we are subject to the turbulence life brings, like a ship at sea with no rudder. Paul writes that we need to "grow up" (Ephesians 4:15). And what is *growing up* in Christ? It's adopting the belief *and* faith in Him that, ultimately, allows us to stop worrying, stop comparing, and stop envying. It's coming to a point where we can patiently trust God to join us in this forest of life—and clear the way.

What We Hope For
It is sometimes difficult to believe in, much less *trust* in, what we can't verify with our senses. Ancient writers knew this would be a challenge for us just as it was for many of them. They encourage us to have assurance despite our *lack of vision*.

Now faith is confidence in what we hope for and
assurance about what we do not see.

— Hebrews 11:1

Thankfully, just because we cannot see God doesn't mean we can't experience His presence and influence. There are countless times in my life in which He showed a very real *appearance* through answered prayers, *un*answered prayers, and not-so-likely *coincidences.* But our confidence should not stop at simply believing that God exists. We should trust in His love, commitment, power, and influence in our lives. It's this very influence that we *hope* for.

> *For I know the plans I have for you, declares the Lord, plans to prosper you and not to harm you, plans to give you hope and a future.*

> —— Jeremiah 29:11

However, hope for a prosperous future doesn't make us impervious to difficulties. The verse in Jeremiah can seem reassuring when we experience minor challenges in life. But how can we hope for prosperity and protection when we're impoverished and injured? What feeling of expectation can we have when the darkness seems overwhelming? Bad things will happen, problems will come. Even so, we must trust that God is still in loving control.

Storms of Life

On November 22, 1873, while crossing the Atlantic Ocean, the steamship *Ville du Havre* struck another vessel and quickly began to sink. One of its passengers, Anna Spafford, found herself in an unimaginably terrifying situation, trying to save her four young daughters as the ocean swallowed the doomed ship. She would survive the ordeal but, tragically, all four girls would succumb to the depths. Days later, Anna's husband and father of the deceased girls, Horatio Spafford, embarked on that same journey across the Atlantic to meet his heartbroken wife. As the ship passed near the place that catastrophe had struck just days before, Horatio was overcome with emotion. There, staring into the sea that held so much of what he loved, he wrote a poem that still resonates:

When peace, like a river, attendeth my way,
When sorrows like sea billows roll;
Whatever my lot, Thou hast taught me to say,
It is well, it is well with my soul.

Though Satan should buffet, though trials should come,
Let this blest assurance control,
That Christ hath regarded my helpless estate,
And hath shed His own blood for my soul (Jenkins 2013).

Though experiencing an inconceivable sorrow, Horatio chose to rest in the assurance of what he could not see. He had hoped his family would safely cross the Atlantic. But now, when his expectation was not met, he still maintained his trust—his firm belief in the reliability, truth, and power of Christ. This is what faith does. It strengthens us, gives us *peace beyond understanding* (Philippians 4:6).

*Hope*fully, most of us will not have to face such a horrible fate. Nonetheless, we can hold tightly to the faith that we are lovingly safeguarded by the Almighty. No matter what comes our way, we can trust that the only way to diverge from our divine destiny is to lose faith.

*Trust in the Lord with all your heart, and do not lean
on your own understanding.
In all your ways acknowledge him,
and he will make straight your paths.*

— Proverbs 3:5-6

The Solution

We All Have It

We all have faith. Everyone, even the most adamant rejecters of religion and God, trusts.

One of my most cherished friends is an adamant agnostic named West. We've been pals for decades now and, despite our many differences, I will always have an immense love for him. Over the years, our conflicting perspectives have sparked multiple challenging, yet fruitful, conversations on polarizing topics like religion, politics, and more. In 2020, when the COVID-19 pandemic struck the nation, West was among the first to embrace the vaccines made available to the public. I, on the other hand, was extremely skeptical. When West and I spoke on the issue, he made an interesting comment—that he "trusted" the medical professionals involved with the development and dispersion of the vaccines. In other words, although West did not have faith in a deity/God, he was very much a man of *faith*.

What differentiated us was in whom that faith was applied. He had full confidence that the injection was beneficial, trusting that the specialists behind the manufacturing, testing, and distribution of the vaccine were acting in his best interests. I, on the other hand, trusted my God-given immunity. Although a relatively trifling topic, I offer this story to illuminate how we are *all* people of faith. We all trust—and direct that trust in someone or something every day in both minor and significant aspects of life.

I don't bring up such a controversial matter to stir up debate. I'm certainly not suggesting we ignore sound medical counsel. It's important to impart our faith responsibly, intellectually, and *hope*fully. To ignore all the advice of our educated, hardworking, and God-given healthcare professionals would be foolish. However, we must also recognize and appreciate the love and power of God. As mentioned in earlier chapters, it is *divine discernment* that helps us navigate such decisions.

Water off a Ducks Back

One day, while attending Texas A&M University, I found myself sitting, ashamed, in the office of a well-respected professor. Moments before I had lashed out at him in what can only be described as a grotesque display of unjustified impertinence. I had lost my temper. Once I calmed down and mustered up the courage to genuinely apologize for my juvenile outburst, he calmly stated "It's ok. It's water off a duck's back." Although I had heard the cliché before, I had not yet fully understood its meaning. Now, sitting in humiliation, I welcomed the implication. He was extending grace, forgiving me without retort. This is what faith does. When we have full confidence that God is looking out for us, that every part of our life is part of His direction for us, offenses are inconsequential. Just like bullets that bounce off the chest of our favorite superhero, forgiveness becomes laughably easy when criticisms can't hurt. When we have faith, the infringements we experience in life become *water off a duck's back*. They quickly enter our lives and exit just as swiftly.

Even today, years later, I appreciate that professor's *faith*.

Trusting BIG

In life, we will all face debilitating challenges. A frightening diagnosis, a devastating loss, the heartbreaking dissolution of a relationship, and more. Tragedy on a grand scale is unavoidable. It is in such times that we must trust *big*. When the mountain seems too tall or the valley too deep, our faith may need to find a new level. Trusting God in a big way can counter big problems, and put peace on the other side of tragedy. The apostle Paul knew this and instructed us to "pray about everything"—even those situations that may feel too overwhelming to be alleviated by something as *seemingly* superficial as trust. But faith is not superficial. It's not just an insignificant, self-soothing tool that we use to trick ourselves into a passive state of mind. Faith unleashes God's infinite power, the same power that created the unfathomable universe. Faith is the catalyst that gives us God's permission to change not only us, but dire situations.

In December of 1981, a Houston woman named Dodie was diagnosed with terminal liver cancer. She was forty-eight and told she had only weeks to live. She and her husband decided to forgo chemotherapy and, instead, go home and pray. For the next several weeks, Dodie and her family prayed fervently and remained optimistic, despite the grim outcome doctors had claimed was unavoidable. More than 40 years later, Dodie was still alive and well, having beaten cancer. She has outlived her husband *and* the doctor who gave her the original diagnosis (McCarthy 2021).

Nothing is impossible with God. We should always seek Him first, even in the most harrowing of circumstances. However, we shouldn't pack away our trust and save it for only calamitous events. Faith should not be a "for emergency use only" resource. We should enable trust for the small things in life as well.

Trusting SMALL

In college, I would never pray to "win" a race. I thought that asking the Almighty for something so trivial was disrespectful and shallow, especially considering the extent of *actual* problems in the world. I would only pray that He "let coach be happy" with my performance. I figured that was a happy medium between involving God in my life as an athlete and not asking too much. However, we are not called to differentiate what issues are worthy of prayer and those that are not. Again, we're told to pray about *everything*, even the seemingly small stuff—and there is good reason for this. God cares about *every* part of our lives. He loves us so much that He wants to be involved in all that we are.

As a father, I enjoy helping my children. My daughter, McKinlee, enjoys making jewelry—like the ring you see me wearing on the front cover. In the past, she has sometimes struggled to get a piece of wire to bend a certain way. I am elated when she asks me for assistance. It brings me sincere joy when I can help my children in even the most trivial way. How much more does our heavenly Father find joy in helping us with the seemingly little things? It's not just ok to pray for a good deal at the grocery store, or that your favorite item is in stock, or even for a little rain for your tomato plants. He *wants* you to. He wants to be included in all of it—every detail. Just like a loving father, if it is important to you, it's important to Him.

But some people, as I once did, will find such requests petty. That's because we think in limits and capacities. Our understanding of the world has trained us to consider resources as finite. Yes, there is terrible suffering in the world that is, in many ways, far more crucial than what flavor of pie we get for the house party. We should always be willing to listen and act on the divine direction to offer healing to those who are hurting. But God doesn't operate with an involvement threshold. He has unlimited bandwidth. He can use His power to help those suffering *and* help us find a great parking space. He wants to help … and it's good to ask.

Night Vision

Night-vision goggles (NVGs) have been used by militaries across the world for more than fifty years. An incredibly useful tool, they allow visualization of images in relatively low levels of light. In nighttime warfare, if their enemy does not have access to the same technology, a military using NVGs will have clear advantages. Can you imagine an entire army being blindfolded and forced to battle an enemy that can see *everything*? Talk about an unfair fight! But this is what *we* do every day.

There are forces outside of our view that are at war. We live on the battlefield. However, we don't have *night vision*, so to speak. Though we can't see the attacks, they are coming moment by moment. They come against our relationships, our confidence, our hope, our ambition, and every other aspect of who we are. The enemy is deceptive and proficient, so much so that we often deny their very existence! This leaves us stranded alone on the battlefield, ignorant of the devastation coming our way. But make no mistake, we are in the crosshairs of invisible enemy snipers. This is why faith is so important. Trust in God unleashes powerful allies against those that seek to destroy us—those dark, invisible forces hellbent on wrecking our lives. Ancient authors were aware of this unseen war.

> *Put on the full armor of God, so that you can take your stand against the devil's schemes. For our struggle is not against flesh and blood, but against the rulers, against the authorities, against the powers of this dark world and against the spiritual forces of evil in the heavenly realms.*
>
> — Ephesians 6:11-12

We may not have NVGs, but it is important that we understand the battlefield that we are on. When we know the enemy is there—even if we can't see them—we can call on the most elite force in the universe to fight on our behalf. Faith is a shield ... and the ultimate weapon.

It May Not Be Easy

God wants what is best for us all. Even though we often derail ourselves, He has the unlimited grace to consistently reroute us back toward that purpose. We should have faith in our access to a loving God who will guide us. But we should not believe that such guidance will lead to an easy life. In fact, it's often the opposite. Following our divine path might be more difficult than we would expect.

Dietrich Bonhoeffer was a German Lutheran pastor, theologian, and anti-Nazi dissident who was hanged by the Nazis after being held prisoner for almost two years. Viktor Frankl, the Austrian psychiatrist who survived years in the Auschwitz-Birkenau concentration camp, witnessed countless doomed prisoners marched to the gas chambers "with the Lord's Prayer or the Shema Yisrael on [their] lips." (Frankl 2006) According to written traditions and biblical accounts, eight of the original Apostles were killed as martyrs, with at least two of them crucified (Peter and Andrew). Paul, who wrote the majority of the New Testament, was beheaded by the Romans. *Do these sound like easy lives?*

Thankfully, God's divine path for everyone isn't martyrdom. For many of us, it means simply abandoning our selfish ambitions and welcoming a life of service. But to have full faith in God is to trust Him completely—even with your life—and committing to this level of trust requires more than just believing. If this news is troubling, that's good. It means you can see the line in the sand, the threshold that must be crossed to put trust entirely in the hands of God. You can choose to step over that line, or not.

When Christ calls a man, He bids him come and die.

— Dietrich Bonhoeffer

Don't Fight It

Trust in the Lord with all your heart,
and do not lean on your own understanding.

— Proverbs 3:5

Not long ago, one of our pet pigs (yes, we have two) got his hoof caught in a large piece of fencing that had fallen over in our backyard. Spanky made it very clear how unhappy he was at being immobilized. He wasn't in pain, but he couldn't walk either, since the wire constricted his leg every time he tried to move forward. With Spanky's ear-piercing grunts and squeals in my face, I knelt and tried to push him backward, out of the fencing. However, something interesting happened when I attempted to push him. He pushed back! For some reason, each time I began to force Spanky backward, he became thoroughly convinced that he needed to go forward. Of course, this didn't help his situation. For a moment, I thought maybe it was because I was standing in front of him that made him react this way. So, I moved to his rear, wrapped my hands around his chest, and tried to pull him backward. But again, that didn't work. The more I tried to get Spanky to move backward, the more aggressively he fought to move forward, exacerbating the problem.

There is a powerful lesson to learn from Spanky's debacle. Many times in life, we will find ourselves *stuck*, snared by self-doubt, anxiety, depression, envy, addiction, or some other immobilizing mindset. Then, we prolong or even exacerbate the situation by ignoring the divine assistance freely offered. We stubbornly fight against God, resisting

Him when He tries to pull us out. We don't like being pushed (or pulled). Ultimately, that's what faith is about. It's a trust that He is in command, that His nudging will lead us in the right direction. We must learn to trust those small detours, those delays or inhibitions we face in life—because they just might be divinely inspired.

Ours, Not Theirs

I stood casually next to him, two men gazing into the fire that illuminated the green hayfield against the dark night sky. It was a cool night in October of 2022. Andrew and I were alone, conversing mildly as the large crowd at the Halloween celebration buzzed in the distance. Per the usual, I was inquisitive, wanting to know more about the man I had just met. As we spoke, I learned that he had worked diligently in the oilfields of West Texas and had built an industrial empire. Andrew was a tycoon, owning multiple businesses that, in total, put his net worth in the tens of millions. He wasn't the least bit pompous, but his status as one of the elites among local entrepreneurs radiated. Something within me churned.

It was déjà vu.

A decade before, I had met a man in similar circumstances—gazing into a different fire on another cool night, listening as the host painted a picture of exorbitant wealth and grandeur. At that time, I had been mesmerized by the allure of it all. I had been willing to do anything to taste that "success", even go so far as to quit the professorship I was so passionate about, uproot my comfortable family, and move to the bareness of West Texas.

219

But now, standing next to Andrew—tempered by a decade of poor decisions and many lessons learned—I was not so malleable. I had learned to trust God, to have faith in His plan for my life. I wasn't called, at least not at that time, to be a multimillionaire. My divine purpose was to be a present father, loving husband, encouraging co-worker, and hopeful author. I could no longer be led away from God to chase selfish, childish dreams. I had been through the valley of comparison—and learned that greed and envy are weapons of self-destruction. I had also let God speak to me through *Extreme Ownership* and listened to my daughter explain the Body of Christ. I had been through the *process*. Standing alongside my new friend, I was a very different person. I knew he and I were on very different trajectories … and I was on the one designed for me. Moses wandered the desert for forty years hoping to find his place in the world. It took me ten.

#Winning

Having faith means that we can confidently live out our divine purpose and not concern ourselves with others. It's trusting that no matter what anyone else says or does, we can boldly move forward. Let others take whatever path they want—but don't follow them.

Theirs is not yours; yours is not theirs.

Encouragement

God knows that life is sometimes difficult. He knows you hurt, you worry, and you cry. He knows the crippling effects of depression, anxiety, and bitterness. He knows you sometimes lose hope—wondering what went wrong—thinking that life isn't supposed to be this way.

This is why faith is so important.

When we are struggling, when the wires of life aren't bending the right way, we have a choice. We can hold on, or relinquish control.

When we can't piece the relationship back together, quit the addiction, or rid ourselves of depression—we need to hand it over. We must loosen our grip and let God take control. Just like my daughter knows that I want her ring to come out perfect, and my son knows that I want his bicycle to function flawlessly, God has our best interests in mind. When He sees our struggles—the pain, the frustration—He wants to help. But He loves us too much to force anything on us. We must choose to have enough faith to hand our problems completely to Him. We must trust—let go—and let God.

Believing in God's plan for your life, and your ability to live it, is what makes all the lessons outlined in *It's a Process* actionable. Because we trust in our divine purpose, we can be honest, humble, and tolerant. It's faith that can justify our kindness and work ethic. We can take ownership because we know the path outlined for us is unique. We can also love without condition, trusting that we, too, are loved in the same way. We can put away the anxiety that constantly attempts to permeate our thoughts, having unbridled faith in our wonderful creator.

Faith makes it possible to experience the abundant, fulfilling life God has planned for you.

Faith makes it possible to really *live*.

CLOSURE

It's a Process, as you now know, is more than a lackluster proponent of decency. It's a plan of attack to counter our tendency to overemphasize the trivial and downplay the paramount—a strategy for fighting the dark forces that would convince us to reject the divine path God has created. The lessons outlined are more than suggestions. They are necessary to carry out the rebellion against our juvenile propensities and the adversary that seeks to destroy us. Although it's not easy to wage war against such a powerful, entrenched enemy, it's one worth fighting—our very soul depends on it.

I know that a desire for purpose stirs within you. It churns like a machine, trying to extract meaning among the excess of bothersome disturbances. You want to be loved, appreciated, and recognized. You hope to find peace and joy. However, sometimes it seems your circumstances will not let that happen. You feel like you will never get there. The good news is that there is indeed *good news*.

Jesus referred to God as "Our Father" (Matthew 6:9)— not only His Father, but *ours*. He is a protector, counselor, and provider available to *you*. And like a loving Father, He gives you the freedom to live life on your terms.

You can work through life trying to create meaning through childish and futile efforts, or embrace the traits and principles that will allow you to discover your *divine* purpose. The choice is entirely yours.

Friend, your mission is one of a kind. You have a detailed assignment, one unlike anyone else in history. But you can't realize it on your own. You must seek God to find it—to live it. Remove the distractions.

Keep praying, learning, and listening. It may not be easy, but it is worth the commitment.

It's a Process.

ACKNOWLEDGEMENTS

First and foremost, thank you to my wonderful wife, Lauren, and my two magnificent children, McKinlee and Lauchlan. I love you more than you know.

I also want to thank all the people who have poured positivity into me over the years: my peeps from Rankin, San Angelo, College Station, Seguin, Midland, Odessa, my CrossFit family, and more. Many of you will never know the extent to which you have inspired me. I love you all.

Lastly, thank you to all those who fought in the writing trenches with me. This book would not have been possible without you.

The trench fighters:

- Brigham Nielsen (encourager)
- Christine Bald (encourager)
- Daniel Lincoln (beta reader)
- Eric Greenhall (encourager)
- Eugenia Greer (beta reader)
- Joanne Katende (beta reader/editor)
- Joseph P. Hamelin (encourager)
- Lauren Dean (beta reader/editor)
- Molly Willcox (writing coach)
- Peter Letzelter-Smith (editor)
- Tammie Mentzel (beta reader)
- Tim Arnold (encourager)

IT'S A PROCESS

SUGGESTED READINGS

- ➤ Bonhoeffer: Pastor, Martyr, Prophet, Spy – By Eric Metaxas
- ➤ Chasing Excellence: A Story About Building the World's Fittest Athletes – By Ben Bergeron
- ➤ Crazy Faith: It's Only Crazy Until It Happens – By Michael Todd
- ➤ Ego Is the Enemy – By Ryan Holiday
- ➤ Extreme Ownership: How U.S. Navy SEALs Lead and Win – By Jocko Willink and Leif Babin
- ➤ How Much More? – By Molly Willcox
- ➤ I Declare: 31 Promises to Speak Over Your Life – By Joel Osteen
- ➤ Lead with AND: The Secret to Resilience and Results in a Polarized World – By Tim Arnold
- ➤ Make Your Bed: Little Things That Can Change Your Life...And Maybe the World – By Admiral William H. McRaven
- ➤ Man's Search for Meaning – By Viktor Frankl
- ➤ The Case for Christ: A Journalist's Personal Investigation of the Evidence for Jesus – By Lee Strobel
- ➤ Winning the War in Your Mind: Change Your Thinking, Change Your Life – By Craig Groeschel
- ➤ Workaholics: The Respectable Addicts – By Barbara Killinger

IT'S A PROCESS

BIBLIOGRAPHY

Barabási, Albert-László. 2018. *The Formula: The Universal Laws of Success.* New York: Little, Brown and Company.

Beaven-Marks, Kate. 2018. "Hypnosis Tips: How to Get Someone Out of Hypnosis (How to Wake People Up)." YouTube Video, October 16, 2018. https://www.youtube.com/watch?v=HJPP1Qozn_0.

Bergeron, Ben. 2017. *Chasing Excellence: A Story About Building the World's Fittest Athletes.* San Bernardino: Lioncrest Publishing.

Bloomquist, Bret. 2007. "Div. II: It's Different." *Track & Field News,* April 11, 2007.

Burton, Tara Isabella. 2017. "The Prosperity Gospel, Explained: Why Joel Osteen Believes That Prayer Can Make You Rich." Vox, September 1, 2017. https://www.vox.com/identities/2017/9/1/15951874/prosperity-gospel-explained-why-joel-osteen-believes-prayer-can-make-you-rich-trump.

Celebrity Net Worth. n.d. "Sam Walton Net Worth." Accessed December 8, 2022. https://www.celebritynetworth.com/richest-businessmen/ceos/sam-walton-net-worth/.

Covey, Stephen R. 2013. *The 7 Habits of Highly Effective People: Powerful Lessons in Personal Change.* New York: Simon & Schuster.

Frankl, Viktor E. 2006. *Man's Search for Meaning.* Boston: Beacon Press.

Graham, Benjamin. 2005. *The Intelligent Investor: The Classic Text on Value Investing.* New York: Harper Business.

Grenfell, Bernard Pyne. 2018. *New Classical Fragments: And Other Greek and Latin Papyri* (Classic Reprint). London: Forgotten Books.

Groeschel, Craig. 2021. *Winning the War in Your Mind: Change Your Thinking, Change Your Life.* Grand Rapids: Zondervan.

Holiday, Ryan. 2016. *Ego Is the Enemy.* New York: Portfolio.

Jenkins, Ferrell. 2013. "Horatio G. Spafford: 'It Is Well With My Soul.'" February 19, 2013. https://ferrelljenkins.blog/2013/02/19/horatio-g-spafford-it-is-well-with-my-soul/.

Keller, Timothy. 2014. [Facebook Post]. Facebook, September 19, 2014.

Killinger, Barbara. 1991. *Workaholics: The Respectable Addicts.* Toronto: Key Porter Books.

Lewis, C. S. 2015. *Mere Christianity.* San Fransisco: HarperOne.

———. 1945. *The Great Divorce.* London: Geoffrey Bles.

Lyall, Sarah. 2007. "In Stetson or Wig, He's Hard to Pin Down." *New York Times*, November 4, 2007. https://www.nytimes.com/2007/11/04/movies/moviesspecial/04lyal.html.

Lyrics.com. 2022. "The Beautiful People Lyrics." https://www.lyrics.com/lyric/3392015/Marilyn+Manson/The+Beautiful+People.

McCahill, Laurence. 2013. "I Wish I Spent More Time in the Office." Medium, August 5, 2013. https://medium.com/the-happy-startup-school/i-wished-id-spent-more-time-in-the-office-90877547da53#.

McCarthy, Anne. 2021. "TV Preacher Joel Osteen's Mom Dodie, 87, Says Prayer Has Kept Her Alive After Cancer Diagnosis 40 Years Ago." SurvivorNet, February 28, 2021. https://www.survivornet.com/ articles/tv-preacher-joel-osteens-mom-dodie-87-says-prayer-has-kept-her-alive-after-cancer-diagnosis-40-years-ago%E2%80%A8/.

McRaven, William H. 2017. *Make Your Bed: Little Things That Can Change Your Life … And Maybe the World.* New York: Grand Central Publishing.

Metaxas, Eric. 2010. *Bonhoeffer: Pastor, Martyr, Prophet, Spy.* Nashville: Thomas Nelson.

Muller, Joann. 2006. "The Impatient Mr. Ghosn." *Forbes*, May 5, 2006. https://www.forbes.com/forbes/2006/0522/104.html?sh=2fe483f127d5.

OfficialHoophall. 2012. "Dennis Rodman's Basketball Hall of Fame Enshrinement Speech." YouTube Video, February 17, 2012. https://www.youtube.com/watch?v=uwbl15Ucl8s.

Reeves, Scott. 2005. "Addicted to Work for All the Wrong Reasons." NBC News, November 18, 2005. https://www.nbcnews.com/id/wbna10099138.

Sterner, Doug. n.d. "Awards: Brian Chontosh." The Hall of Valor Project. Accessed December 14, 2022. https://valor.militarytimes.com/hero/3632.

Tchekmedyian, Alene. 2014. "Burbank Couple Honored for Saving Toddler Who Fell Out of Third-Story Window." *Los Angeles Times,* April 1, 2014. https://www.latimes.com/socal/burbank-leader/news/tn-blr-burbank-couple-honored-for-saving-toddler-who-fell-out-thirdstory-window-20140401-story.html.

Wilcox, Molly. 2022. *How Much More?* Waterford: United House
        Publishing.

It's a Process

Made in the USA
Monee, IL
04 January 2023